Ralph Emerson Twitchell

Ralph Emerson Twitchell

The Historian
Who Found
New Mexico's
Future
in the Past

Daniel Jason Twitchell

SUNSTONE
PRESS

SANTA FE

Sunstone books may be purchased for educational, business, or sales promotional use.
For information please write: Special Markets Department, Sunstone Press,
P.O. Box 2321, Santa Fe, New Mexico 87504-2321.

Book and cover design › Vicki Ahl
Body typeface › Minion Pro
Printed on acid-free paper
∞

Library of Congress Cataloging-in-Publication Data

Names: Twitchell, Daniel Jason, 1979- author.
Title: Ralph Emerson Twitchell : the historian who found New Mexico's future
   in the past / by Daniel Jason Twitchell.
Other titles: Historian who found New Mexico's future in the past
Description: Santa Fe, NM : Sunstone Press, [2017] | Includes bibliographical
   references.
Identifiers: LCCN 2017046838 | ISBN 9781632932051 (softcover : alk. paper)
Subjects: LCSH: Twitchell, Ralph Emerson, 1859-1925. | Historians--United
   States--Biography. | Historians--New Mexico--Biography. | Lawyers--New
   Mexico--Biography. | Politicians--New Mexico--Biography. | New
   Mexico--Biography.
Classification: LCC E175.5.T95 A3 2017 | DDC 907.2/092 [B] --dc23
LC record available at https://lccn.loc.gov/2017046838

SUNSTONE PRESS IS COMMITTED TO MINIMIZING OUR ENVIRONMENTAL IMPACT ON THE PLANET. THE PAPER USED IN THIS BOOK IS
FROM RESPONSIBLY MANAGED FORESTS. OUR PRINTER HAS RECEIVED CHAIN OF CUSTODY (COC) CERTIFICATION FROM: THE FOREST
STEWARDSHIP COUNCIL™ (FSC®), PROGRAMME FOR THE ENDORSEMENT OF FOREST CERTIFICATION™ (PEFC™), AND THE SUSTAINABLE
FORESTRY INITIATIVE® (SFI®). THE FSC® COUNCIL IS A NON-PROFIT ORGANIZATION, PROMOTING THE ENVIRONMENTALLY
APPROPRIATE, SOCIALLY BENEFICIAL AND ECONOMICALLY VIABLE MANAGEMENT OF THE WORLD'S FORESTS. FSC® CERTIFICATION IS
RECOGNIZED INTERNATIONALLY AS A RIGOROUS ENVIRONMENTAL AND SOCIAL STANDARD FOR RESPONSIBLE FOREST MANAGEMENT.

WWW.SUNSTONEPRESS.COM
SUNSTONE PRESS / POST OFFICE BOX 2321 / SANTA FE, NM 87504-2321 /USA
(505) 988-4418 / ORDERS ONLY (800) 243-5644 / FAX (505) 988-1025

Dedication

For my grandmother, Virginia Ruth Twitchell

Drawing of Ralph Emerson Twitchell by the Author.

Contents

8

Acknowledgements

Throughout the course of constructing this manuscript I was aided by an array of individuals and agencies, and I am pleased to offer all of them the recognition they so richly deserve.

The primary resource utilized in amassing information for this project was the New Mexico State Library. The Southwest Collection, and the State Records Center and Archives proved invaluable, and the personnel staffing both were always forthcoming with assistance. The Fray Angelico Chavez History Library, and the Thomas C. Donnelly Library also yielded useful material, as did the City of Las Vegas Museum and Rough Rider Memorial Collection.

A number of individuals devoted time and energy to this work. Foremost among them was Kristie Ross, PhD, whose guidance and editorial expertise improved the quality of this manuscript. I would also like to thank Peter Linder, Tom Ward, and Steven Williams, PhDs all, for their support and encouragement. Additionally, Stella Mason is due a nod of recognition. Thank you all for your help.

My parents, Wirt and Barbara Twitchell, deserve a special thank you; I could not have done this without them.

Finally, I wish to express my eternal gratitude to Melissa Newfield, who has been my most ardent supporter.

Preface

Ralph Emerson Twitchell was one of the most important and enigmatic figures in early New Mexico history. Twitchell was a prominent lawyer, politician, writer, and promoter who had a tremendous influence on New Mexico. He was among the group of talented individuals who migrated to the territory in the late nineteenth century, but he managed to distinguish himself from the rest—as an attorney, a public speaker, and as an author. Twitchell was one of New Mexico's leading citizens for over four decades, a pillar of the community, and a devoted civil servant. Yet, he is also one of the least known and understudied public figures in the state's history. This book examines Twitchell's influence on New Mexico, filling in the existing gaps in the historical record, and giving Twitchell the credit he deserves as one of the fathers of modern New Mexico. The sources consulted for this project include the books and personal correspondence of Twitchell himself, historical monographs covering a variety of New Mexico subjects, the relevant general histories, a number of newspapers and websites, and extensive archival materials.

Introduction

Ralph Emerson Twitchell was a distinguished American legist, statesman, publicist, historian, and philanthropist whose astute foresight, practical ingenuity and aggressive acquisitiveness had a profound influence on New Mexico. He was an intelligent, intuitive, and audacious individual whose many notable accomplishments excited notice in his contemporaries as well as subsequent generations. In addition to being at least partly responsible for transforming Santa Fe into a tourist Mecca, he was a prominent personage in New Mexico's fight for statehood. As a legal practitioner he helped establish a portion of the state's juridical criterion and was involved in the adjudication of countless cases both as an emissary of the government and as a representative of private interests. When unoccupied with professional and civic obligations R. E. Twitchell spent much of his time working on various literary endeavors. Over a span of more than three decades he authored countless works, most relating to New Mexico. These ranged in scope from multi-volume historical disquisitions that set the standard for historiography in the region, to single-paged promotional pamphlets that helped reinvigorate the stifled economy by recasting New Mexico as a haven for vacationers.

Still and all, Twitchell was much more than the sum of his accomplishments. He was a dynamic, complicated figure who struggled to reconcile his own interests with his self-conscious sense of civic responsibility and the amoral demands of his profession. Bold, deliberate and highly motivated when impassioned with intent, R. E. Twitchell was unafraid of instigating controversy, and capable of inciting resentful animosity in his adversaries. His apparent disregard for the concerns, opinions, and positions of others periodically engendered a great deal of hostility, and over time garnered him numerous enemies, some of whom were important individuals within his own political party. Conversely, to those who called him friend Twitchell was extremely loyal. When it came to his country, to his political party, and to his employer R. E. Twitchell truly had no reservations about choosing fealty over personal advantage.

A complicated figure to say the least, R. E. Twitchell defies simple explanation. This may be why he has not up to this point been the subject of extensive historical examination. That a man with Twitchell's resume has been passed over by historians for so long is baffling. What is it about the complexity of his character that has made him such an historical enigma?

When Ralph Emerson Twitchell first came to the New Mexico Territory in 1883, the region was a wild and unruly place where political corruption and lawlessness ran rampant. A collection of powerful Republican land speculators, businessmen, lawyers, and politicians known as the "Santa Fe Ring" allegedly controlled the territory, influencing and manipulating both its political and judicial proceedings. William Henry McCarty, also called William H. Bonney, and better known as "Billy the Kid," New Mexico's most infamous malefactor had only recently been assassinated, a scapegoat for the violence perpetrated during the Lincoln County War. Also Geronimo, the notorious Chiricahua Apache chieftain, was still mounting incursions along New Mexico's southern border and inciting insurrection within portions of the area's autochthonous population. New Mexico had been a territory of the United States for roughly 30 years, and most Americans at the time ignorantly considered the province to be a barren, utterly worthless wasteland on the periphery of the nation. Unfavorable descriptions of New Mexico had branded the territory as a primitive, moisture-starved expanse of desolate terrain. This unfortunate depiction persisted long after the United States acquired New Mexico and distorted many Americans' views about the region. Seen as an arid void principally populated by foreigners and Catholics, it was derided as a culturally backward place where disputes were settled by gunfire and national political oversight was nominal at best.

Despite its questionable public image, the New Mexico Territory guarded vast mineral wealth, the hint of which attracted a number of capable, industrious and enterprising individuals. Some of these entrepreneurial spirits enriched themselves by participating in the development of the region's many untapped resources. Others capitalized on the boom and bust economies characteristic of the exploitative wave of commerce that accompanied the extraction industries. Most of them failed miserably in their endeavors and found that they had to scratch a living out of an unforgiving landscape. But those who prospered found that their affluence and influence enabled them to direct the development of the burgeoning territory.

Ralph Emerson Twitchell was among those intrepid souls who journeyed to the desert southwest in search of fortune and esteem. A native of the midwest, Colonel Twitchell immigrated to New Mexico Territory late in the nineteenth century and then rapidly became a leader and luminary within his adopted home. Fortuitously, Twitchell arrived in the nascent region at an opportune time to participate in the political and economic revamping already underway. The developing territory afforded him ample prospects for success, and Twitchell deftly maneuvered himself into favorable situations time and again. This habit ultimately set him on a trajectory to become one of New Mexico's most influential historians and illustrious patrons.

Like a majority of the wayfarers that made their way to the American Southwest in the late 1800s, Ralph Emerson Twitchell was a fiercely independent and self-reliant individual. Physically, he was an imposing man, tall and robust with a handsome visage and a thunderous speaking voice, traits that meant at times he could be dictatorial and recalcitrant. But he was generally considered a well-mannered gentleman with a dignified demeanor that masked an underlying conviviality.

After landing in the New Mexico Territory, Ralph Emerson Twitchell quickly established a reputation as an adroit trial lawyer while working for the Atchison, Topeka and Santa Fe Railroad Company. Over time his scores of professional successes garnered him increasing prestige and sparked a rise to prominence within the community. His elevated stature in turn led to further opportunities for political and professional advancement.

Mindful of the fortuity of his circumstances, Colonel Twitchell parleyed his talents into a number of high-level appointments within the territorial government and a sound career as an elected official. In well under a decade, Ralph Emerson Twitchell went from newcomer to power-player. He then used his status and his various positions of authority to affect change within his community.

A masterful politician, Twitchell was able to convince others to support him through persuasive oration and inveiglement, talents that ensured his opinion would be taken into account when administrative decisions had to be made. He became a dynamic force in New Mexico politics and influenced some of the most important and momentous events in the region's history. Twitchell was instrumental in New Mexico's transition from territorial status to statehood and Santa Fe's transformation from a defunct overland shipping center to a premiere vacation destination. Additionally, R. E. Twitchell also had a hand in reviving one of the social traditions of the region, the annual Fiesta celebration that takes place every autumn in New Mexico's capital. Above all else, public service was Ralph Emerson Twitchell's true forte. He possessed a highly developed social conscience and a great deal of ambition that compelled him to serve his country politically, militarily, and legally. He proved a highly effective politician, capable of assuaging concerns and winning people over without resorting to pandering or quid pro quo arrangements. He also possessed an uncanny ability to appeal to uninformed constituents without condescension. Twitchell held a variety of public offices and enjoyed a long career as a civic leader, a role that he took extremely seriously. He even served as a soldier in the militia of his adoptive home to fulfill his perceived civic responsibility. All told, his tenure as a civil servant spanned nearly half a century and left an indelible mark on New Mexico.

But Ralph Emerson Twitchell's political accolades, professional distinctions, and civic accomplishments tell only part of his story. Colonel Twitchell was a complex, multi-faceted individual with myriad interests. In addition to being an accomplished lawyer and a dedicated statesman, Twitchell was also a craftsman and builder as well as the author of several monographs covering various epochs in New Mexico history. His contemporaries considered him an authority on the region's past and his Leading Facts of New Mexico History is still one of the seminal works in New Mexico historiography. Furthermore, Colonel Twitchell was an accomplished archivist who worked indefatigably to assemble and secure a valuable collection of historically significant documents for posterity.

However industrious, R. E. Twitchell was an undeniably congenial man who led a vibrant social life. He belonged to several fraternal associations and a variety of benevolent organizations, a number of which he ultimately led. These included the Masons, the Elks Lodge, the Historical Society of New Mexico, and the New Mexico State Museum, as well as many others.

In short, Ralph Emerson Twitchell worked hard to cultivate general prosperity in the southwest, both for himself and for the rest of the region's populace. A fervent proponent of all things New Mexico, Colonel Twitchell was an impassioned spokesperson for the area. He advocated for the development of its resources and expounded endlessly on the beauty of its landscape. He promoted the architecture of the region as the only uniquely American building style and championed the history of New Mexico as an important, nationally relevant supplement to the country's East Coast creation myth. His unbounded pride in New Mexico even led Twitchell to take on the role of peregrinating publicist, on several occasions traveling across the country to campaign for his adopted home.

Like other notable turn of the twentieth century New Mexicans, such as Thomas Benton Catron or Frank and Charles Springer, Colonel R. E. Twitchell was a gutsy, resourceful, and well-educated gentleman with an iron will and an unquenchable desire to succeed. A true renaissance man, Colonel Twitchell had his hands in nearly everything he could reach. His lasting contributions as a public figure, lawyer, politician, historian, scholar, publicist, and philanthropist define him as a man of extreme efficacy, while the personal and professional relationships he forged with some of the most notable men in the country reveal him to be a man of eminence and distinction.

Yet, despite his prominence and his many accomplishments, Ralph Emerson Twitchell remains an enigmatic historical figure who has been largely overlooked by chroniclers. Little has been written about Colonel Twitchell since his death in 1926, and that which has amounts to little more than the events of his life swaddled in the mythos that grows out of nostalgia. Beyond the trite, anecdotal sycophantism that characterizes most accounts of Ralph Emerson Twitchell's life, questions remain about this Midwestern transplant with ties to some of the most powerful people in the country. Was he really the benevolent altruist that he appears to have been in retrospect? Perhaps he was merely a self-interested opportunist whose ostensive generosity was simply a means to an end. Could he have been some sort of aggregate of the two? At times R. E. Twitchell was most certainly an aggressive developer who advanced his objectives even in the face of controversy or outright hostility. However, he was also a major patron of the arts in Santa Fe and an ardent devotee of New Mexico. In short, reconciling all the disparate aspects of his personality and accomplishments is difficult to do.

Information supporting any of these arguments can be easily acquired. While most of the existing data reinforces the image of Ralph Emerson Twitchell as a noble-minded benefactor, some evidence suggests there was a connection between him and the notorious "Santa Fe Ring," an association that could conceivably sully R. E. Twitchell's reputation by implicating him in some of "The Ring's" more nefarious transgressions. Further muddying the waters with disreputability is scandalous evidence implicating Twitchell in some unethical land dealings.

While he was most likely neither miscreant nor saint, Colonel Ralph

Emerson Twitchell was assuredly a man of pith and substance, who for about two score years around the turn of the twentieth century, was a force to be reckoned with in the American Southwest. He may have skirted the periphery of impropriety from time to time in order to achieve his aims, but even in those instances where R. E. Twitchell's conduct could be questioned (such as the time he exhibited footage of the Taos Corn Dance against the wishes of tribal leaders), at no time was he motivated by malicious intent. This lack of malice does not excuse his missteps, but it does lend some perspective, casting Twitchell as single-minded in the pursuit of his agenda rather than as a hateful and abhorrent villain. Whatever his indiscretions, Twitchell played an integral role in shaping both the reality and the perception of New Mexico at a crucial time in the region's history.

The indelible mark left on New Mexico by Colonel Ralph Emerson Twitchell is indisputable but difficult to quantify. Twitchell was not a Promethean figure that rescued New Mexico and its inhabitants from primordial darkness. Twitchell was a cog in a machine whose feats amount to a share of the New Mexican gestalt. While he was a catalyst in the emergence of modern New Mexico, he did not accomplish his exploits in a vacuum; a great many other important and influential individuals also contributed to the cultural and economic evolution of New Mexico. Within the context of the territory's progression from a frontier community into the forty-eighth State in the Union, R. E. Twitchell was just one of many individuals deserving credit for the reshaping. However, even as a member of a coalition, Twitchell stood out from the rest of the pack, driven to the front by an unshakable belief in the civic responsibilities of the privileged. His contributions, affirmed by the enduring legacies of intellectual development, cultural resurrection and economic prosperity, persist in New Mexico to this day.

In this essay I examine Colonel Ralph Emerson Twitchell's role in the Americanization of the city of Santa Fe, the State of New Mexico, and the entire southwestern United States. As previously noted there have been remarkably few texts written about Colonel Twitchell, but the reservoir of knowledge concerning him is by no means dry. R. E. Twitchell's own literary works, The Bench and Bar of New Mexico During the American Occupation, A.D. 1846–1850, History of the Military Occupation of the Territory of New Mexico from 1846 to 1851 by the Government of the United States, and The Leading Facts of New Mexico History: Volumes 1-5, as well as The Spanish Archives of New Mexico, Spanish

Colonization in New Mexico in the Onate and De Vargas Periods, Dr. Josiah Gregg: Historian of the Santa Fe Trail, Old Santa Fe, and the Genealogy of the Twitchell Family, provide a wealth of information about his family and personal life, as well as insight into his psyche.[1]

The New Mexico State Record Center and Archives in Santa Fe houses court records that bear Twitchell's name, in addition to several collections that include information relating to Twitchell, and a stockpile of Twitchell's personal and professional papers. The L. Bradford Prince Papers, and the J. K. Shishkin Collection both contain pertinent newspaper clippings, and the R. E. Twitchell Collection is filled with correspondence, legal documents, and an assortment of newspaper articles, essays, and obituaries relating to the events of his life. Additionally, the State Record Center and Archives houses the Territorial Archives of New Mexico, which also contains material pertaining to Twitchell.[2] While no definitive biography of Colonel R. E. Twitchell exists, a number of biographical adumbrations, loaded with details about his life, can be found in the historical journals Arizona and the West and The New Mexico Historical Review, which make up part of the Southwest Collection at the New Mexico State Library. The Southwest Collection also contains the newspaper reference book Representative New Mexicans, that profiled Twitchell in 1912, and El Palacio, and The Santa Fe Magazine, which are full of relevant reference material.[3] A collection similar to the one housed at the New Mexico State Records Center and Archives, containing familial correspondence, several of Twitchell's speeches, and an abundance of newspaper clippings, is housed in the Fray Angelico Chavez History Library in Santa Fe, NM.[4] Additionally, the Special Collections department of the Donnelly Library at New Mexico Highlands University in Las Vegas, NM includes four books containing information pertaining to R. E. Twitchell: Telling New Mexico: A New History, New Mexico: A Brief Multi-History, Illustrated History of New Mexico, and History of New Mexico: Its Resources and People. The Donnelly Library also houses a master's thesis, Four Gentlemen Historians of New Mexico, which contains information about R. E. Twitchell.[5]

In addition, information related to Twitchell can be found in several general history books on New Mexico and the Southwest, including Hubert Howe Bankcroft and Henry Ebbeus Oak's History of Arizona and New Mexico 1530–1888, Warren A. Beck's New Mexico: A History of Four Centuries, Thomas E. Chavez's New Mexico Past and Future, Charles F. Coan's A History of New

Mexico, Myra Ellen Jenkins' A Brief History of New Mexico, L. Bradford Prince's A Concise History of New Mexico, and Frank Driver Reeve's History of New Mexico. Supplemental information can be found in other more specific texts on New Mexico such as New Mexico: A Biographical Dictionary 1540–1980 by Don Bullis, New Mexican Lives: Profiles and Historical Stories by Richard W. Etulian, The Story of New Mexico: Its History and Government by George Peter Hammond, A History of New Mexican-Plains Indian Relations by Charles L. Kenner, Santa Fe: The Autobiography of a Southwestern Town by Oliver La Farge, Yesterday in Santa Fe: Episodes in a Turbulent History by Marc Simmons, Early Railroad Days in New Mexico by Henry Allen Tice, Santa Fe: A Modern History by Henry J. Tobias and Charles E. Woodhouse, and The Far Southwest 1846–1912: A Territorial History by Howard R. Lamar.[6]

Twitchell is also mentioned in several historical monographs. The biographies, Thomas Benton Catron and His Era by Victor Westphall, and Frank Springer and New Mexico: From the Colfax County War to the Emergence of Modern Santa Fe by David L. Caffey contain useful information, as does the personal memoir of Governor Miguel Otero, My Nine Years as Governor of the Territory of New Mexico 1897–1906. Chasing the Santa Fe Ring: Power and Privilege in Territorial New Mexico also by David L. Caffey, and Forty-Seventh Star: New Mexico's Struggle for Statehood by David V. Holtby also include information pertaining to Twitchell and New Mexico.[7]

The historical reader New Mexico, Past and Present edited by Richard N. Ellis includes essays relevant to Ralph Twitchell as well. New Mexico's fight for statehood and the Santa Fe Ring are two of the subjects covered that provide contextual information surrounding Twitchell's activities. This compilation even includes an essay by R. E. Twitchell himself covering the conquest of New Mexico by American forces that provides insight into his perspective as an Anglo-American author in early twentieth century New Mexico.[8]

Innumerable newspapers from around the country also printed stories about Twitchell. His name appeared regularly in the various New Mexico newspapers for close to forty years. NewspaperArchives.com afforded access to these periodicals.

This essay is divided into ten chapters and an epilogue. The first chapter recounts the details of Ralph Twitchell's family history, childhood, education, and his immigration to New Mexico. Chapter Two describes the conditions in New

Mexico at the time of Twitchell's arrival and covers the commencement of his political career and military service, as well as his start as a civil servant. Aspects of
his personal life are also explored. Chapter Three focuses on Twitchell's work as a
railroad attorney. The fourth chapter examines the years R. E. Twitchell served as
the district attorney of the First Judicial District of the Territory of New Mexico.
Chapter Five relates the specifics of Ralph Twitchell's term as the mayor of Santa
Fe. Chapter Six outlines Twitchell's political career, concentrating on his role as
an orator. The particulars of his various wartime contributions are also included.
Chapter Seven details R. E. Twitchell's efforts to transform Santa Fe into one of
the world's premiere tourist destinations. The eighth chapter delves into the promotion and patronage Twitchell provided the state of New Mexico. Chapter Nine
covers Twitchell's many literary endeavors. The tenth and final chapter recounts
Twitchell's last days, as well as the particulars of his funeral. The epilogue looks at
the public response to Twitchell's death.

This recounting of the life of Ralph Emerson Twitchell offers the most
complete examination of this important historical figure to date. Necessitated
by the glaring lack of recognition given such an important historical personage,
this project draws Twitchell out of historical obscurity and establishes him in his
rightful place amid history's most influential New Mexicans.

1

Self-Consciously Twitchell

"A people that take no pride in the noble achievements of remote ancestors will never achieve anything worthy to be remembered with pride by remote descendants."
—Macaulay[9]

The transcendentalist writer Nathaniel Hawthorne once wrote, "Families are always rising and falling in America." This concept of an unfixed and fluid society perfectly articulates the socio-cultural zeitgeist of nineteenth-century patrician America, and highlights the egotistic self-awareness with which upper-class Americans defined themselves. To the genteel, the family name was a weighty thing, laden with all the accomplishments and transgressions of one's ancestors. The wrong relation could mean the difference between acceptance and exclusion in prominent social circles so it was important to maintain the honor of one's family. Like many other nineteenth-century American aristocrats, Ralph Emerson Twitchell subscribed to this ethos. His sense of personal identity was constructed upon its conceptual framework.

Ralph E. Twitchell belonged to an old and distinguished family with roots extending back across the Atlantic Ocean to England. As was the case with many of his contemporaries, Twitchell was extremely interested in who he was and where he came from, not only biologically but also in a cultural sense. In an effort to answer these questions, he began working on an exhaustive family genealogy, an endeavor he pursued steadfastly until illness dictated he lay down his pen. As the undertaking progressed, Twitchell discovered that genealogists in New England had already tenuously traced his lineage back to the time of William the Conqueror. Twitchell was, however, unwilling to accept this distinguished pedigree at face value. He continued his research and was able to ascertain that the supposed link tracing his family name back to the time of the Norman invader amounted to little more than speculation and conjecture. The grand claims concerning this imagined lineage were just lofty assertions that could not be confirmed.

Because of a popular fad of the times, pronouncements of this kind concerning one's ancestry were not all that uncommon. By the late nineteenth century it had become fashionable for Americans with European roots to dredge up (or contrive) links to old world aristocracies to impart some semblance of nobility to their family names. However, Twitchell gave very little credence to that canard. He saw no need for apotheosized European kinship ties in the United States, where hereditary title stood for very little. Also, unlike many of his con-temporaries, R. E. Twitchell refused to accept a theoretical or imagined ancestry just because it bestowed an assumed honor or merit. He scoffed at status seekers who attempted to aggrandize their surnames with old world titular distinctions, believing instead that a simple homesteading heritage was more in keeping with America's ancestral ideals and the character of its Puritan ancestors.[10]

Plainly stated, Twitchell didn't require any European distinctions to determine his exceptionality. Indeed, he regarded his essential Americanness as the fundamental imperative that defined his existence. Twitchell saw himself and his family as entirely American and the United States as the legacy of his ancestors. For those reasons he focused on his American rather than his English ancestry. However, he did not ignore his Anglo-Saxon heritage altogether. In spite of his personal bias, Twitchell did trace his family line all the way back to his Britannic forbearers. His research yielded an ancestral lineage tracing back to an Englishman named Benjamin Twitchell, who had settled in the Massachusetts Bay Colony in the early seventeenth century.[11] Along with his older brother Joseph, Benjamin Twitchell first brought the family surname across the Atlantic. From these brothers, R. E. Twitchell was able to trace his ancestry back almost two centuries to 1460 and the birth of a Henry Twitchell in Chesham, England, which is the earliest substantiated record of the family name.[12] Ultimately, his discoveries undermined or at the very least, cast serious doubt upon the previous suppositions concerning his noble ancestry. However, his search also resulted in the replacement of his supposedly highborn pedigree with a lineage he consid-ered no less respectable, a bloodline infused with the Puritan ethic that Twitchell gratifyingly referred to as a "sturdy yeoman pedigree."[13]

With these somewhat more humble beginnings as the cornerstone of his genealogical foundation, Ralph Twitchell turned his attention back to the descen-dants of Benjamin Twitchell and his direct family line. He uncovered evidence pointing to his progenitors being both industrious and shrewd, qualities that allowed them to flourish in pre-Revolutionary America. The data he compiled suggests that the Twitchell family enjoyed favorable social standing in all the communities in which they dwelt. Whenever members of the Twitchell family were mentioned in documents from colonial New England, each of the individual's names was prefaced with the title, "Gentleman."[14]

Twitchell had always been a well-respected appellation on the American continent. Early records highlight a number of highly esteemed personages who bore the name. A member of the Twitchell family is listed among the "fathers of the town" of Lancaster, Massachusetts, and a number of other Twitchells attained distinction as husbandmen, surgeons, or artisans.[15] Additionally, several Twitchells distinguished themselves as persons of consequence within the political arena. One member of the family was even elevated to the status of folk hero in a section of New England. His name was Ginery Twitchell, the cousin of R. E. Twitchell's grandfather. During the 1840s, he was celebrated by the residents in and around Worcester, Massachusetts as an unrivalled express rider.[16]

Ralph Twitchell's research into his ancestral background made one thing apparent. Differentiating oneself from the rest of the population through excellence and service to one's country was a Twitchell family tradition. This familial characteristic was aptly evinced by the Twitchells who took up arms to liberate the American colonies from British tyranny. From the outset of the Revolution, Twitchells served the cause of American independence. Twitchells were among the "minutemen" that were the first to respond to the alarms sounded for the defense of Lexington and Concord on April 19, 1775, and several members of the family willingly gave their lives during the protracted conflict.[17] R. E. Twitchell's great-grandfather Daniel Twitchell served in the Continental Army for the entirety of the war. He first saw action at the Battle of Lexington as a private in Capt. Samuel Lamson's company of militia, and later distinguished himself at the famous Battle of Bunker Hill by remaining on the field until the engagement's final moments in an attempt to keep a cannon from falling into the hands of British forces.[18] While not all Twitchells found glory on the field of battle the way Daniel Twitchell did, every member of the Twitchell clan in North America was a staunch supporter of the American Revolution. In fact, "there is no record or intimation that a solitary descendant of Benjamin Twitchell was a Tory or sympathized in any way with the Loyalists."[19] For such a thoroughly American individual like R. E. Twitchell, this must have been extremely pleasing information to uncover.

In the wake of the American Revolution, the Twitchell family proliferated and moved beyond the confines of New England. By 1833, the year that Ralph Twitchell's father was born, Twitchells were established throughout the Union. As the frontier moved further and further West, Twitchells moved with it, always in the vanguard of American expansion.

R. E. Twitchell's genealogical investigations eventually led to his own grandparents, Jonas and Sara Ellen Weekes Twitchell, whom he wrote of as having been endowed with the "pioneering spirit so general in the early American families in the history of our country."[20] Jonas Twitchell and his family, including several small children, migrated from Vermont to Scio Township in Washtenaw County, Michigan in 1830. There, in the shadow of Ann Arbor, Ralph Emerson Twitchell's father Daniel Sawin Twitchell was born three years later.

The seventh of eight children, though only the fourth to survive past infancy, Daniel Sawin Twitchell grew up laboring on his family's farm. Life was difficult on the rugged Michigan frontier and his youth was filled with countless hardships. When he reached adulthood, Daniel S. Twitchell entered Oberlin College in Ohio. He did not graduate, however. After a brief stay at Oberlin he returned to Michigan intent on pursuing a legal career. He immediately enrolled at the University of Michigan, and four years later was a member of the first class to be graduated from that institution's law department.[21a]

After receiving his law degree Daniel S. Twitchell felt that it was time to settle down. In 1858, he married Delia Scott, the daughter of English immigrants from Northumberland. The couple wasted little time in starting a family. Just a year after their nuptials, on November 29, 1859 they became the parents of a baby boy. The child was named Ralph Emerson Twitchell, presumably after the "Sage of Concord" Ralph Waldo Emerson. Their decision would prove to be prescient, as R. E. Twitchell later displayed a tremendous aptitude for writing and scholarship.[21b]

The year of Ralph Emerson Twitchell's birth was one of the most contentious in the nation's history. The Union his forefathers had helped to secure and develop was on the verge of a great schism. The future of the "peculiar institution" of slavery was being furiously debated, and civil war loomed ominously on the horizon. In 1860 the situation grew even more dire, and before the year's end South Carolina had declared that it was seceding from the Union. Ten other states followed shortly thereafter and the United States was soon at war with itself.

The conflict escalated throughout 1861, and as the casualties began to mount, Americans grew increasingly concerned with the toll that the war was taking. Several members of the Twitchell family plunged into the fray, but Daniel Sawin elected not to go off to war. With an infant son at home and his wife already pregnant with another child, he had more immediate concerns than the war. On October 30, 1861, following the news of a Confederate victory at Ball's Bluff, Delia Twitchell gave birth to the couple's second son, whom they named Wirt Beecher Twitchell.21c

By the end of 1862, Daniel and Delia Twitchell were preparing to add one more to their brood. Barely a year after the birth of their second child they welcomed a baby girl into their family. The new arrival was given the name Luella Scott Twitchell in matronymic tribute to her mother's lineage. Sadly, she died while still an infant.[22]

Ann Arbor, Michigan remained the family's home until the conclusion of the Civil War. Following the war the Twitchells removed to Kansas City, Missouri.[23] Before the close of 1865 they had found their way to one of Kansas City's rooming establishments, the Southern Hotel, where young Ralph and his little brother entertained themselves cutting capers on the staircase.[24]

Two years later, the Twitchell family was still growing accustomed to life in Missouri when tragedy struck. In July 1867, Delia Scott Twitchell died from an unspecified malady. Shortly thereafter, Daniel Sawin Twitchell married Mary Benjamin, an intelligent young woman who was unfazed by the prospect of having to raise two prepubescent boys. From the outset, Mary wholeheartedly embraced caring for her stepchildren, and did her best to fill the void left by their mother's death. She nurtured and guided Ralph and Wirt, molding them into ethical, up-standing citizens.[25]

While his sons thrived under the tutelage of their new stepmother, Daniel Sawin Twitchell went on to become a celebrated attorney and an individual of note in Kansas City. He held several public offices during a long career in civil service, and is credited with being "one of the men who promoted the best interests of Kansas City during the period of foundation laying."[26]

When they were old enough, Ralph and Wirt were enrolled in Kansas City's public school system.[27] In addition to being a capable student Ralph proved to be a gifted athlete. In high school "he threw a wicked baseball" pitching for the Kansas City High baseball team, leading them to victory.[28] After graduating from high school in 1877, Ralph chose to attend college in Lawrence, Kansas.[29] The University of Kansas was relatively close to home, but far enough away that it afforded a level of independence to the young man. While studying at K. U., Twitchell was recruited to play for the university's baseball team.[30] He was also known to be a bit of a prankster who enjoyed engaging in hi-jinks with his friends. His antics eventually led to his suspension from school for thirty days, after he and his friends carried out an elaborate hoax involving the University's Chancellor and a member of the Board of Regents.[31] The incident proved too much for R. E. Twitchell's father to tolerate. Believing that his son had been involved in too much foolishness at K. U., Twitchell's father withdrew him from the University and sent him to Michigan to complete his education.[32] Ralph Twitchell returned to Ann Arbor, somewhat humbled and refocused academically, intent on earning an LL.B. from the University of Michigan. A diligent and astute pupil this time around, young Ralph Twitchell excelled in law school and impressed the faculty so much that he would later be invited back as a guest lecturer. He graduated in 1882 and thereafter turned his attention to the west where there were plenty of opportunities to ply his newly acquired trade. [33]

After obtaining a degree R. E. Twitchell returned to Kansas City, Missouri, where "he was admitted to the bar and acted as assistant to the city counselor" for a brief period of time.[34] In the spring of 1883, Twitchell relocated to Las Vegas, New Mexico to serve as an assistant to Judge Henry L. Waldo, the solicitor for the Atchison, Topeka and Santa Fe Railroad Company.[35] Judge Waldo was a well-connected figure within New Mexico with ties to the region's most influential people. He was also the most respected lawyer in the territory.[36] As far as opportunity for professional advancement was concerned, R. E. Twitchell could not have been in a better situation.

Presumably, R. E. Twitchell relocated to New Mexico because of the plethora of opportunities taking shape throughout the territory as a result of eastern corporations investing in industries such as railroads and mining.[37] However, a distant relative, Ginery Batchelor Twitchell (the famous equestrian postal carrier) had served as the sixth president of the Atchison, Topeka and Santa Fe Railroad during its infancy, approximately a decade prior to R. E. Twitchell's arrival in the territory.[38] This kinship may have played a role in Twitchell's decision to migrate to the Southwest, but there is no indication that he received his job with the A.

T. & S. F. Railroad Company because of his relation's former position within the organization.

R. E. Twitchell arrived in the New Mexico Territory when the high-desert landscape was locked in winter's icy embrace. Fittingly, he came via steam engine, the quintessential nineteenth-century symbol of progress. The nation's rail network had grown so extensive by the early 1880s that he was able to traverse the vast expanse of the Great Plains entirely by locomotive, although he probably had to switch trains several times along the way because the country had not yet adopted a standardized rail gauge. Twitchell's arrival produced little fanfare. However, he quickly made a favorable impression on the area's residents. Shortly after his arrival The New Mexican described him in an editorial as "a pleasant young gentlemen of excellent social qualities and fine legal attainments."[39] Clearly, some in New Mexico perceived Twitchell as having enormous potential. Yet, in the years to come, he would exceed even their grandest expectations.

2

NEW MEXICO

"Without exception there was no town which harbored a more disreputable
gang of desperadoes and outlaws than did Las Vegas"
—Ralph Emerson Twitchell

I n the late nineteenth-century America's western states and territories offered a
wealth of opportunities to anyone with enough courage to brave the hardships
and deprivations of frontier living. Prospects for success began to balloon
throughout the region in the aftermath of the Civil War, when corporate interests
both foreign and domestic began pouring money into the West to capitalize on
the region's burgeoning agricultural and mineralogical industries. This spate
of capital investment created a host of jobs in secluded places and generated a
massive influx of people into isolated quadrants of the map. Additionally, the
federal, territorial, and state governments proffered land grants as incentives
to companies willing to build railroads in order to bolster the nation's shipping
and transportation infrastructure. Railroads made the peripheral portions of
the United States more easily accessible, and integrated them more fully into the
expanding national and international markets. The railroads also generated inci-
dental economic opportunities through the enterprises attached to the industry,
which enticed even more people to migrate to the region.

Several railroad companies began laying track across New Mexico in the last
quarter of the nineteenth century, thereby reducing its isolation from the rest of
the nation. However, ignorance, disorder, and criminality prevailed in the region,
and the leading industry, mining, was exceedingly speculative. Furthermore, New
Mexico was a political backwater with limited interest in attaining statehood.[40] It
was relatively lawless, a dangerous and unpredictable place where nothing could
be counted on as a certainty. However, it also harbored endless possibilities to
acquire wealth and renown for industrious individuals.

Perhaps Ralph Emerson Twitchell was responding to the siren song of
frontier riches when he chose New Mexico as the place to make his way. Although,

given his predilection for civil service, as well as his self-imposed obligation to contribute to the expansion and improvement of the country, it is likely that the unruly conditions in New Mexico held their own allure for Twitchell. Rowdy and undeveloped, but growing rapidly, New Mexico presented optimal circumstances for the ambitious young man. Opportunities to build up American civilization abounded throughout the territory. It was an ideal locale for Twitchell to distinguish himself and carry on the pioneering tradition of his ancestors.

Not long after his move to New Mexico, Twitchell got his first opportunity to participate in the Americanization of the Southwestern frontier. In 1884, less than two years after his arrival in the territory, Twitchell was offered a commission as aide de camp on the staff of Governor Lionel Allen Sheldon with the rank of Major in the volunteer militia of the Territory of New Mexico.[41] He gladly accepted. The position made Twitchell an assistant to the chief executive of the territory. In the year that followed, Twitchell became a valued member of Governor Sheldon's staff. He developed a good rapport with territorial officials, and grew increasingly comfortable mingling with influential New Mexicans. The prominent position Twitchell longed for, felt he deserved, and was destined to fill seemed to be coming within his reach, and he had only been in the territory for a matter of months.

Then in 1885, a new territorial governor was appointed: Edmund G. Ross, a former senator from Kansas. A Democrat, the new governor fired Twitchell and replaced him with a subordinate loyal to his own administration. Twitchell was, however, unfazed by the apparent ebbing of his political potential. He simply found other means of involving himself in territorial politics. That year Twitchell proposed the formation of a new militia company in Santa Fe.[42] The impetuous and calculating young man was audacious enough to suggest that the administration allocate funds to support another contingent of soldiers while the new governor was still acquainting himself with the office. It was a bold move, given his youth and Republican affiliation, but Twitchell was not afraid of overstepping his bounds. He was supremely confident in his assessment of the militia's needs, and having been a military advisor to the previous governor he felt qualified to make recommendations on military matters. The move was Twitchell's bid to remain among the territory's decision-makers, and it worked. Recognizing Twitchell's proposal as sound, or perhaps just growing weary of the young man's persistence, Governor Ross approved the plan to expand the militia. Twitchell was then tasked with organizing the new militiamen.[43] Nonetheless, he was far from the governor's inner circle and was actually regarded as a thorn in his side.[44]

In 1885, R. E. Twitchell also participated in his first military action. He was detailed for duty in a campaign against one of the region's Native American tribes and served on the staff of Major Adna Chaffee, Sixth U.S. Cavalry. His company scouted in Sierra and Grant Counties in pursuit of renegade Apache Indians from the San Carlos Indian Agency. While in the field Twitchell also acted as inspector for Governor Ross. His work with the territorial militia had obviously convinced the governor of his competence regarding military concerns.[45]

This expedition thrust Twitchell into the middle of a momentous historical event; the group absconding from the San Carlos Indian Reservation was led by none other than Geronimo, the infamous Chiricahua Apache resistance fighter. Though Twitchell played a relatively unimportant role in the manhunt, he was among those sent to corral the "Scourge of the Southwest" in one of the best known operations of the Apache Wars. Committed to the assimilation of New Mexico's Native American population, Twitchell had no qualms about participating in the apprehension of such a famous symbol of Native American resistance. His vision for New Mexico as a modern, commercial, fully Americanized region required the integration of the Native population. Furthermore, Twitchell was proud of contributing to the "civilization" of the frontier. He was also proud of holding the rank of Major, and was pleased to contribute to his family's already storied military heritage. For Twitchell, this military service represented the first step toward fulfilling his self-imposed duty to preserve and protect the country his ancestors helped establish and sustain.

The surrender of Geronimo and his followers marked the end of armed Amerindian insurrection in the Southwest. From that point, the whole region was under the control of the United States government. Symbolically, it was a tremendous milestone for the country. The United States had successfully consolidated its power throughout the vast reaches of its southwestern section. In actuality, however, the incarceration of an aging chieftain and his miniscule band of starving warriors did little to quell the lawlessness that plagued the territory. New Mexico remained a rough, violent locale filled with bandits, gunmen, bunko artists, confidence men, prostitutes, and all manner of murderous marauders. These nefarious elements would have to be eliminated, or at the very least reduced, if New Mexico was going to become anything more than a treasure-trove to be plundered. Simply put, Euro-Americans were not looking to raise families in an underdeveloped expanse of rustic wilderness teeming with bloodthirsty desperadoes. While New Mexico was not quite that wholly disreputable and anarchic, the prevailing image of the territory at the end of the nineteenth century was one of disorder and chaos. Heavily embellished dime novels touting the exploits of William Bonney (Billy the Kid) and his ilk had made the territory infamous for violent acts during the 1870s. The variety of felonious transgressors inhabiting the area, taking advantage of the limited scope of law enforcement in the country's hinterlands had been transformed into romantic literary antiheros. Thieves and murderers were recast as rebels and iconoclasts. Combating the violence that led to this perception was vitally important if the territory was going to be rendered suitable for Euro-American families and welcomed into the Union. That meant subduing or ejecting New Mexico's colorful assortment of malevolent scoundrels, an initiative R. E. Twitchell whole-heartedly embraced. Not only because it was good for his employer, the Atchison, Topeka, & Santa Fe Railroad, and for the development of the territory, but for personal reasons as well. Twenty-five years old in 1885, Twitchell was thinking about marriage and family himself. A safer environment in which to raise his prospective brood would be in his best interests.

Contemptuous of passivity, Twitchell did not simply ruminate over society's woes he played an active part in the removal of New Mexico's criminal element when presented with the opportunity, despite the fact that he was not a law enforcement officer. On one occasion in 1885, Twitchell, acting on behalf of his employer, journeyed to the town of Belen to expose and apprehend some underhanded individuals who were preying on the rail company's customers in that area. A gang of con artists, thieves, and pickpockets had been operating out of the burgeoning village for several weeks, taking advantage of the opportunity presented by a newly constructed railroad installation. Upon arriving in Belen, Twitchell found the iniquitous crew and quickly ascertained that a "hulking troglodyte" named Wilson was the group's headman. He promptly took the scoundrel into custody and brought him before the local authorities. While the proper affidavit was being drawn up in the offices of the local justice, Wilson grew irate and destroyed the town's only copy of the territorial statutes. Perhaps, he believed that without the books he could not be convicted of the crimes with which he was being charged. This was not an entirely asinine theory considering the volumes contained the ordinances, regulations, and codes used to administer justice in the territory. Their absence could delay any attempt to convict and incarcerate him. However, Twitchell was unfazed by the inflammatory act and simply shipped the offender off to the town of Los Lunas to await trial.[46] Having successfully beheaded the criminal enterprise Twitchell returned to Santa Fe, undoubtedly gratified at reducing the number of criminals on New Mexico's streets, if only by one.

Exploits such as this audacious capture, which was reported in the territorial newspapers, made many New Mexicans take notice of the brazen young man from Kansas City. He was already establishing a reputation as a top-notch lawyer among attorneys and courtroom officials; now, people throughout the territory were learning his name, and more importantly, associating it with the rule of law. Before long, Twitchell would seek to capitalize on his growing reputation, but at the time he was preoccupied with his personal life. He wanted to get married and have children. The wild and unpredictable nature of the territory did nothing to discourage this impulse. In 1885, he became engaged to Margaret Olivia Collins, "a prominent society belle of St. Joseph, Missouri."[47] Like R. E. Twitchell, Ms. Collins came from an eminent mid-western family. She was a frontier debutante, and by all accounts an enchanting woman with a pleasant and amiable disposition.[48] The couple's parents most likely arranged their union. Twitchell's father still resided in Missouri, near the bride's hometown and was probably responsible for pairing off his son with the local beauty. Perhaps arranging for his son to get married was Daniel Sawin's way of attempting to curb his son's reckless behavior. Regardless of what brought Ralph and Margaret together, the pair appears to have been well matched. They sought out each other's company whenever they had the opportunity, crisscrossing the plains to spend special occasions and holidays together during their engagement. However, Twitchell's personal concerns took precedence over his professional aspirations only briefly, because in 1885 he was also promoted to assistant attorney for the A. T. & S. F. RR. This new position demanded most of Twitchell's time, but as 1885 was drawing to a close he managed to pull himself away from his work long enough to marry. R. E. Twitchell and Margaret Collins were wed on December 9, 1885 in St. Joseph, Missouri.[49]

Chief San Juan (Mescalero Apache), Margaret Olivia Collins and Ralph E. Twitchell,
Tertio-Millennial Exposition, Santa Fe, New Mexico, 1883.
Courtesy of the Palace of the Governors Photo Archives (NMHM/DCA), #011241

Following their nuptials Mr. and Mrs. Twitchell took up residence in Santa Fe. They moved into a home a few blocks north of the plaza that had previously been occupied by powerful Republican boss Thomas Catron.[50] The couple was able to live comfortably, enjoying financial security thanks to R. E. Twitchell's new position within the A. T. & S. F. They enjoyed socializing and threw lavish parties entertaining their many friends.[51] Before long the pair were fixtures in Santa Fe high society.

In 1886, pregnancy compelled Mrs. Twitchell to return to Missouri in preparation for giving birth. Unfortunately, while with child Mrs. Twitchell fell gravely ill.[52] She eventually recovered from the ailment but would suffer intermittently from poor health throughout the rest of her life. Any concerns about the effect her illness might have had on the unborn child were assuaged when Mr. and Mrs. Twitchell enjoyed the blessing of a healthy son on January 20, 1887. They named the child Waldo Collins Twitchell. The moniker may have stemmed from R. E. Twitchell's own namesake Ralph Waldo Emerson. However, given the closeness of the relationship that Twitchell shared with Judge Henry Waldo, the boy could have been named after this treasured friend and mentor.

While the child was still a toddler the family moved to Las Vegas, New Mexico. Raised in the shadow of the Sangre de Cristo Mountains, Waldo grew up strong and able-bodied, in contrast to his mother, who was again seriously ill before the boy's first birthday.[53] As before, Mrs. Twitchell recovered and was able to participate in raising her son for several years following. At the appropriate age, Waldo was enrolled in the public schools of Las Vegas, New Mexico, in the preparatory department of the New Mexico Normal University (currently NMHU).[54] At home Waldo was nurtured, well cared for, and raised with an emphasis on hard work and American idealism. As he grew the boy began to demonstrate the same artistic temperament that R. E. Twitchell possessed, and quickly became a great source of pride to his parents, particularly his father.[55]

As R. E. Twitchell's family grew so too did his power and influence. Over the relatively short period of time he had been in New Mexico, Twitchell had managed to position himself favorably within the territorial Republican Party. He had also become affiliated with many of the most powerful people in the region, including members of that infamous cabal that was rumored to run the territory, the Santa Fe Ring. On top of that, he was one of the preeminent lawyers in the territory. By 1890, just eight years after his arrival in the territory,

R. E. Twitchell had become one of New Mexico's leading citizens.

Confident in the territory's prospects, Twitchell began looking to expand his landholdings. In 1891 the young lawyer presented his wife with a twenty-two acre fruit orchard in the hills east of Espanola.[56] He had decided on the small farm near Santa Cruz after reconnoitering locations across the territory. By late summer the Twitchells were constructing a palatial stone residence on the property.[57] Once completed the house became the family's retreat. It was far too remotely located to serve as a full time residence for the young professional, his socialite wife, and school-aged child, but it was an ideal sanctuary away from the noise and commotion of life in a frontier town.

Having acquired property in the Espanola valley, Twitchell grew increasingly concerned with the development of that region. In his usual fashion, he became an outspoken proponent of progress in the area and began promoting the growth of the nascent "American colony" there.[58] His patronage and desire to develop northern New Mexico continued well into the twentieth century, but lamentably, the farm was not to become the multi-generational estate R. E. Twitchell had envisioned. Within a few years Mrs. Twitchell would require hospitalization, and R. E. Twitchell would sell the idyllic property.

Throughout the 1890s R. E. Twitchell worked hard to provide for his family while advancing his career and fulfilling some of his political aspirations. He also delved into new areas of interest such as writing, an avocation that would turn out to be arguably his most lasting legacy. Indeed, the future looked promising for the young attorney as the twentieth century approached, but in reality all was not well. During the later part of the decade R. E. Twitchell's wife fell victim to an undetermined infirmity that rendered her an invalid for the remainder of her life. When she fell ill, Ralph was forced to sequester her at the state hospital in Las Vegas for care. On January 29, 1900, after a long struggle with the debilitating illness, Margaret Olivia Collins Twitchell died.

Not long after Margaret Twitchell's passing, R. E. Twitchell sent his adolescent son to Kansas City, Missouri to live with his grandparents. Kansas City had become a bustling metropolis by the dawn of the twentieth century, and Ralph probably felt that Waldo would receive a better education there than in a frontier town in the New Mexico Territory. In Missouri, Waldo attended Kansas City Central High School. He then headed north to his father and grandfather's alma mater, the University of Michigan, where he earned a degree in engineering.[59]

After graduating in 1910, Waldo Twitchell moved to Arizona where he worked as the head of the assay department of the Vulture Mines Company for four years. In 1914, he resigned the position and returned to New Mexico to work with his father on the New Mexico Board of Exposition Managers, a body created to represent the state at the Panama-California Exposition, in San Diego, California the following year.[60]

Captain Waldo Twitchell in Uniform, Norfolk, Virginia, 1918. Photographer: Faber Studio. Courtesy of the Palace of the Governors Photo Archives (NMHM/DCA), #013431

Focusing on his legal career, his political aspirations, and his vision for New Mexico, R. E. Twitchell rebounded from the loss of his wife with uncanny celerity. Over the years that followed he met with tremendous professional success, but eventually he came to acknowledge the void left by the loss.

In 1916, Ralph Twitchell married for a second time. His bride was for-ty-nine-year-old Estelle Bennett Burton, a worldly, well-educated woman with considerable literary talent. Originally from Mount Vernon, Iowa, she had been a resident of Las Vegas, New Mexico for a number of years prior to their nuptials. Like R. E. Twitchell, she was Episcopalian and an active participant in civic affairs. She was also "a student and writer of history." Her work had been published in several periodicals, including Old Santa Fe: A Magazine of History, Archaeology, Genealogy, and Biography, edited by Twitchell.[61] Ms. Bennett Burton's skill as a writer and researcher had impressed Ralph Twitchell to such a degree that he enlisted her to assist him with his own historical research. After working together for a couple of years their professional relationship gave way to a romantic en-tanglement.[62] Accordingly, the two decided to get married. Shortly thereafter, R. E. Twitchell and Estelle Bennett Burton were wed in Santa Fe, in a ceremony presided over by the reverend Leonidas W. Smith.[63]

Following their wedding the couple took up residence in Santa Fe. They erected a home a few blocks northwest of the plaza along the verdant Arroyo De Las Mascaras in the "Santa Fe" architectural style. The attractive adobe dwelling featured exposed vigas, monastic walls, and an imposing stone tower that resem-bled a Spanish torreon. About the house, the Twitchells cultivated a sprawling garden that helped make the property one of the most picturesque in the city.[64]

The Twitchells were known to entertain extravagantly in their Santa Fe showplace. Over the course of their ten-year marriage they frequently hosted so-cial gatherings for their friends and neighbors. Though regarded as a serious man whose deportment often bordered on punctilious, R. E. Twitchell was particularly fond of revelry. He delighted in the company of his friends and welcomed any chance to host them at his palatial estate.[65]

Mrs. Ralph E. (Estelle) Twitchell, 1900 – 1910?
Courtesy of the Palace of the Governors Photo Archives (NMHM/DCA), #008037

House of Col. Twitchell, n.d.,
Courtesy of the State Archives of New Mexico, Karl J. Belser Photograph Collection, #8724

House of Col. Twitchell, n.d.,
Courtesy of the State Archives of New Mexico, Karl J. Belser Photograph Collection, #8725

House of Col. Twitchell, n.d.,
Courtesy of the State Archives of New Mexico, Karl J. Belser Photograph Collection, #8726

House of Col. Twitchell, n.d.,
Courtesy of the State Archives of New Mexico, Karl J. Belser Photograph Collection, #8727

House of Col. Twitchell, n.d.,
Courtesy of the State Archives of New Mexico, Karl J. Belser Photograph Collection, #8728

Ralph and Estelle Twitchell were devoted to each other and spent nearly all of their time together. The pair was very interested in the development of Santa Fe and was actively involved in local civic and cultural affairs. They also collaborated on a number of literary endeavors. After R. E. Twitchell's death in 1925, Estelle remained in the stately pueblo-style home that they had built until shortly before her own passing in 1952.[66]

Ralph Twitchell resided in New Mexico for more than forty years. Throughout that time he consistently acted in accordance with what he deemed to be the best interests of the territory/state.

3

Plains, Trains, and Legal Ordeals

*"Do not go where the path may lead, go instead
where there is no path and leave a trail."*
—Ralph Waldo Emerson

The decision to relocate to New Mexico proved to be a lucrative course of action for Ralph Emerson Twitchell. The young attorney flourished in the developing territory, attaining tremendous professional success as legal counsel for the Atchison, Topeka, and Santa Fe Railroad. As it branched out across the Southwest, the rail company engendered innumerable lawsuits, because it periodically impinged on the lives and landholdings of others. When litigation could not be avoided, Twitchell represented the interests of the railway. An exceptional legal mind, Twitchell prevailed in countless courtroom battles, saving the A. T. & S. F. untold sums of money. His record grew so lopsided with victories that it aroused skepticism in some of his more cynical contemporaries. These suspicions notwithstanding, Twitchell's triumphs on behalf of the railroad propelled him to the top of his profession and led to his being offered a variety of appointments in the territorial and national governments. Having arrived in New Mexico as railroad companies were beginning to stretch their lines across the territory, Twitchell was able to capitalize on the industry's expansion. Indeed, the railroads became the wellspring of his success. He made his living and his reputation as a railroad lawyer arguing the right of way of the iron horse, a de facto agent of modernization.

R. E. Twitchell first came to New Mexico to work as an assistant to Henry Waldo, a highly regarded judge and attorney who worked as the chief legal officer for the A. T. & S. F. railroad. Regardless of any professional advantages he may have been able to enjoy in Kansas City (his father was well connected throughout the region), the town was too modern and developed, too cosmopolitan. By the 1880s, the country's western frontier lay far beyond the Missouri River. Had he stayed, Ralph Twitchell would have been unable to play a seminal role in the development of a frontier settlement like so many of his ancestors had done. Judge Waldo's law office offered this crucial element, the opportunity to participate in the development of an American territory, because late nineteenth century New Mexico was still a virtual blank slate with regard to certain aspects of the law. Before Twitchell arrived in New Mexico "no questions in which railway corporations were interested and which were of vital importance to them in operating in the Southwest had been adjudicated by the territorial Supreme Court."[67] These circumstances created a favorable situation for the young lawyer, positioning him to take part in significant lawsuits while still a legal neophyte. Ultimately, Twitchell would be involved in litigating important cases that established legal precedents concerning the operation of railroad companies throughout the region.

The position that brought R. E. Twitchell to New Mexico in 1883 became the foundation of an illustrious legal career. Serving as both employer and mentor, Mora County District Court Judge Henry Waldo completed Twitchell's legal training, instructing him on the finer points of litigation. Under the judge's tutelage, Twitchell showed signs of becoming a particularly skilled legal practitioner. The young attorney had an inherent talent for deliberation, and was a surprisingly polished orator for someone just twenty-four years old. He was also a man of great physical stature with a deep sonorous voice, whose commanding presence could garner the attention of an entire room, an obvious asset in front of any jury. Additionally, Twitchell was extremely thorough, displaying a particular aptitude for conducting research. Recognizing his potential, Waldo began grooming Twitchell to be his successor in the A. T. & S. F.'s legal department.[68]

Judge Waldo provided invaluable guidance and instruction, but he was not the only legal expert who contributed to R. E. Twitchell's legal proficiency. Another courtroom guru in the employ of the railroad, Frank Springer, subsidized the direction Twitchell received from the Judge. Springer was a brilliant barrister from Iowa who had made his way to New Mexico in the early 1870s. He amassed a sterling record of success while practicing law in the territory. Serving as assistant attorney under Judge Waldo, Springer handled 106 cases for the A.T. & S.F. R.R. between 1879 and 1898, with only one courtroom defeat. He was deemed so valuable by the A. T. & S. F. that the company named the newly established rail hub of Springer, New Mexico in his honor. Watching this masterful attorney skillfully manage court proceedings undoubtedly had an impact on Twitchell's own approach in the courtroom.[69]

While working with Judge Waldo, R. E. Twitchell became close friends with both Waldo and Frank Springer. Twitchell and Waldo's friendship spanned more than thirty years, until the Judge's death in 1915. Their paternal bond was so profound that it led Twitchell to immortalize Waldo posthumously in a historical volume he wrote about New Mexico. Moreover, Henry Waldo may have been the namesake of R. E. Twitchell's only son, though that is difficult to substantiate. The relationship Twitchell shared with his colleague Frank Springer also turned out to be a longstanding association marked by mutual esteem and admiration. Beyond the law, the two men had common interests in history and archaeology. Both were members of the Archaeology Institute of America and the Museum of New Mexico. Their connection lasted until Twitchell's death in 1925, and Springer served as one of the honorary pallbearers at Twitchell's funeral.

Working under Judge Waldo, Twitchell was quickly identified as a "powerful pleader and finished speaker," possessing tremendous legal acuity.[70] As such, he was put to work representing the A. T. & S. F. in damage suits. Just months after his arrival, Twitchell was arguing cases throughout the region.[71] After diligently executing his duties for nearly two years, Twitchell was rewarded for his hard work by the railroad's management. In 1885, he was appointed assistant attorney for the company and "thereafter for 29 years he had active charge of the trial, office, executive and administrative legal work of the New Mexico department in the lower and appellate courts of the territory and state, and in the United States Supreme Court."[72]

As assistant attorney for the A. T. & S. F., Twitchell was generally concerned with mitigating damages in litigious land disputes. The railroad displaced a number of people as it laid tracks across the New Mexico territory, and these uprooted individuals, squatters, and legitimate claimants alike frequently filed retributive lawsuits against the company. Twitchell represented the A. T. & S. F. in many of these claims and "proved his value to the railway company in important damage suits" year after year.[73] Over time his case history swelled with favorable judgments on behalf of the railroad, and for many New Mexicans the resonant timbre of his voice became a harbinger of steel rails.

Twitchell and his colleagues working for the A. T. & S. F. under Judge Waldo were so successful in defending the company, that no judgment was recorded against that railroad by the New Mexico Supreme Court until well into the twentieth century. This almost unbelievable record of efficiency aroused some suspicions of impropriety. It even drew a smattering of criticism in the pages of Collier's Weekly, a popular American magazine of literature and journalism. The speculative insinuations that had emerged were never substantiated, however, and Santa Fe's railroad lawyers dismissed the insult without comment.[74]

The countless decisions rendered in Twitchell's favor made him a vital functionary in the A. T. & S. F.'s expansion throughout the region. With the company's growth dependent upon gaining the right of way through lands across the territory, it was of crucial importance to the rail company that they not become mired in protracted court battles. Twitchell's virtually unblemished record in legal proceedings encouraged the railroad's expansion, because it empowered the company to expand their operation without trepidation, secure in the knowledge that Twitchell could mitigate any damages they might incur. This effectively made Twitchell an important ambassador for the territorial faction in support of modernization and American integration. He was now furthering this group's collective efforts with every courtroom victory. By forwarding the interests of the railroad, Twitchell was also satisfying his own desire to see the territory developed.

Due to Twitchell's effectiveness as a litigator, he acquired considerable wealth and benefited from his growing reputation as well. However, Twitchell's legal exploits also caused a great deal of distress and anger. Many times Twitchell represented the company against a plaintiff who had just lost a husband or father in some tragic incident involving the A. T. & S. F. or one of its subsidiaries. In these instances, a victory for Twitchell often times meant a crushing, life-altering defeat for someone's widow or orphaned children. Unfortunately, this was a byproduct of the industrial development of the territory, the victimization of people, casualties of the relentless onslaught of locomotive technology.

Twitchell's record in legal proceedings grew so impressive by the end of the nineteenth century that he began to attract national attention. Even the Attorney General, the head of the Justice Department, noticed his growing reputation. The acclaim led to new professional possibilities for the young lawyer. Private citizens and corporations that encountered legal problems looked to him for representation. He also began to receive overtures proffering attractive positions within the territorial and even the national judicial infrastructure.

In 1898, Ralph Twitchell served as the Attorney General of New Mexico.[75] He also argued at least one civil case and at least one liability suit, all while still on the payroll of the A. T. & S. F. That year he was also elected president of the New Mexico Bar Association. In the latter he succeeded the venerable Albert B. Fall of Las Cruces, and was just the sixteenth man to hold the position. The following year Twitchell was reelected to a second term. At least fifteen years had elapsed since an individual had been elected to consecutive terms as presiding officer. His reelection served as a tangible endorsement from his peers of his skills as a legist.[76]

A year later, in the spring of 1900, R. E. Twitchell was offered an appointment as the United States District Attorney for the Territory of New Mexico. His nomination was supported by no less a personage than Theodore Roosevelt. The prestigious position would have cemented Twitchell as the preeminent lawyer in the territory and would have all but guaranteed him an extended political career. But after much deliberation Twitchell refused the appointment, because it would have meant severing his connections with the A. T. & S. F. railroad. In a letter postmarked December 15, 1900 addressed to Roosevelt, the new Vice Presidential nominee of the Republican Party, Twitchell expressed his gratitude for Roosevelt's support before explaining that he would regrettably not be able accept the position because he was inundated with cases relating to the railroad and was unwilling to abandon the company that had given him his start and treated him so well. Twitchell believed he "would not be treating the railroad company right to desert them"[77] and later explained as much to the Attorney General, John W. Griggs.

The rail company's board of directors rewarded Twitchell's integrity and commitment. In 1907, after years of unwavering loyalty and distinguished service, Twitchell was named Assistant Solicitor for New Mexico for the A. T. & S. F. The promotion was both a reward for a job well done and an inducement to remain in the company's employ. Retaining the services of R. E. Twitchell was an utmost priority for the A. T. & S. F., because there was no one in the territory who could replace him. Twitchell was just too valuable to lose. He held the office of assistant solicitor until 1915, at which point he retired. However, this did not completely end his employment with the organization. He continued to serve the railroad under the title of Special Counsel, a position that freed Twitchell, by that time in his fifties and a highly regarded civil servant, to pursue interests outside of the legal field while remaining at the company's disposal. The A. T. & S. F. continued to call on Twitchell in intricate cases that required his expertise, returning time and again to the reservoir of knowledge that had proved so valuable.[78]

One of the finest lawyers in New Mexico, Twitchell remained at the top of his profession even after taking a step back from the A. T. & S. F. He was still a masterful litigator and his recognized expertise in railroad law made him a unique resource for New Mexico jurists and judicial officials. When contentious legal proceedings involving rail companies arose, Twitchell could be relied upon to provide insight and aid in adjudicating the cases. In the event of an emergency, Twitchell was at the top of the list of possible troubleshooters. His reputation as a legal virtuoso even once prompted a judge to install him in a fiduciary position within a struggling rail line that was deemed vitally important to the economy of central New Mexico. Twitchell was called upon to lend his knowledge and know-how to restoring the foundering company.

In 1917 the New Mexico Central Railroad, a railway line operating in the Estancia valley south of Santa Fe was drowning in a sea of red ink. The company had been struggling for a number of years and was teetering on the brink of collapse. The failure of the railroad would have been a devastating blow to the development of both the burgeoning agricultural district through which it traveled and the city of Santa Fe, which it served. Consequently, the company was deemed too important to the development of New Mexico's interior to be dismantled or allowed to fold.[79] The courts sought to ensure that the faltering rail line maintained its solvency, and the ensuing investigations of the New Mexico Central turned up evidence of fiscal malfeasance. More than six thousand dollars was unaccounted for and appeared to have been misappropriated by the receiver of the railroad, Ralph C. Ely. After failing to account for the missing sum, Ely was removed from his position by District Judge Reed Holloman. The judge then appointed R. E. Twitchell to succeed Ely.[80] Under Twitchell's guidance the New Mexico Central enjoyed a resurgence. He managed to reverse the railroad's fortunes and get them back on track, figuratively speaking. Twitchell held the receivership through 1919, executing the duties of the office with impressive proficiency.[81] When Judge Holloman finally discharged Twitchell as receiver of the railroad, he felt the need "to express his appreciation of the excellent services..." the lawyer had rendered the company. In a newspaper editorial he commended Twitchell, crediting him with demonstrating that the railroad could "be successfully operated and eventually put on a paying basis."[82] Following Twitchell's tenure, the company managed to remain in business for an additional seven years, before being acquired by his longtime employer the A. T. & S. F.

Rescuing the New Mexico Central Railway from bankruptcy and dissolution was a fitting culmination to Twitchell's long career as a successful railroad attorney. His body of work in the field encompassed three decades, and included a series of courtroom victories that aided in the growth of New Mexico's rail infrastructure. After spending almost half his life advocating on behalf of rail companies, both in and out of the courtroom, it was especially fitting that Twitchell cap off his career as a railroad attorney by facilitating the revival of a failing but crucial railway.

Separation from the railroads did little to diminish Ralph Twitchell's caseload however; he remained as highly sought after a lawyer as there was in the Southwest. He continued to practice law for years thereafter, and was ultimately appointed to a high-level legal position within the government. He was even considered for a federal judgeship at one point.[83] Now, Twitchell had zero interest in such an appointment; more than that, he was entirely unwilling to accept the position were it tendered him, and he said as much in a letter he wrote to The Santa Fe New Mexican in response to his name emerging on the list of candidates. His terse announcement stated that under no circumstances would he ever consider accepting the judgeship, and in truth he was absolutely dead set against holding public office.[84] However, the circumstances behind Twitchell's aversion to office holding are a whole different story all together.

4

A Thankless Job

"You are damned if you do, and damned if you don't."
—Ralph Emerson Twitchell[85]

As a representative of the A. T. & S. F. Railroad in contentious land disputes, Ralph E. Twitchell became a high profile character within the New Mexican community. Word of his skill and acumen in the courtroom radiated from Santa Fe and Las Vegas, garnering him a reputation as one of the ablest lawyers in the region, and making him a highly sought after litigator. He enjoyed an almost meteoric rise to prominence, achieving both celebrity and distinction while still in his twenties. His esteem grew until it reached well beyond New Mexico's bench and bar, and his name began to circulate among officials responsible for filling the important legal appointments within the territory's judiciary. Initially, however, commissions within the territorial government were limited for Twitchell, for reasons that had little to do with his legal expertise. Having arrived in New Mexico shortly before the inauguration of a Democratic governor, Twitchell, an outspoken Republican, had few political opportunities during his early years in residence. With the appointment of a new Republican territorial governor in 1889, the political climate turned in his favor and opened new possibilities. Shortly thereafter, Twitchell found himself in the unenviable position of being a political officer in an extremely contentious politically partisan atmosphere. He quickly began to loathe holding public office. Indeed, the experience was so exasperating that it left him somewhat jaded and unsure whether he wished to continue with public service.

Throughout Ralph Twitchell's first five years in residence in New Mexico the young attorney flourished. By 1888, he had a thriving family, a successful law practice, and a social network that included some of New Mexico's most powerful and illustrious citizens. His interactions with the territory's elites had expanded beyond the professional realm. Many now considered him a New Mexican, particularly within the Republican element, who recognized his potential as a valuable political ally. The brilliant young lawyer and his family had been embraced as full-fledged members of the community. In conjunction with his social ascendance, Twitchell developed close friendships with influential New Mexico Republicans like L. Bradford Prince. He also joined a group of fellow Santa Fe attorneys, (also local Republican politicians) in fielding a baseball team. The attorneys/politicians pitted themselves against other assemblages of professional men, including a team of Democrat office holders, who they competed against in a highly publicized contest in 1888. This match-up proved to be an epic duel that resulted in one participant having to be carted off the field with a spinal injury. In the end, just a single run separated the teams. Twitchell and the attorneys prevailed, outlasting the office holders in a high-scoring battle, and seizing bragging rights over their political and professional rivals. Twitchell pitched for his team and preformed well before handing the ball off to teammate Clarence Allan, who closed out the victory. Bested by their opponents, the chagrined collection of Democrats sloughed off the field trying to justify the defeat, upset over their perceived loss of face at the hands of their political adversaries.[86] The significance of the game was exaggerated in the contentious world of nineteenth-century New Mexico politics. As one of the catalysts in the win, Twitchell undoubtedly enjoyed a little stardom in the wake of the victory. The symbolic contest made him a more recognizable figure, even a minor celebrity, but it also made him a high value target for New Mexico Democrats.

In 1889, recently elected Republican President Benjamin Harrison appointed a new territorial governor for New Mexico, and consequently, employment opportunities in the public sector opened for R. E. Twitchell. The new governor was Twitchell's close friend, and political ally L. Bradford Prince, a staunch Republican and a leading member of the "Santa Fe Ring."[87] With a confederate in control of the territory, Twitchell sat at the right hand of the most powerful official in New Mexico. His potential for political advancement skyrocketed, and he looked to be well situated under the new Republican regime. Not only was he a devoted party man, but also he had actively campaigned to secure Prince's confirmation to the governorship.[88] Twitchell was among those earmarked for a commission within the new administration. Some New Mexicans had him slated to be the next secretary of the territory.[89] He was on the cusp of becoming a consequential figure in New Mexico, and no one would have been more aware of it than he.

After taking office in April 1889, the new governor appointed R. E. Twitchell district attorney for the First Judicial District of New Mexico.[90] His close affiliation with Governor Prince aside, Twitchell's legal expertise made him a logical choice to fill a position in the territory's judicial system. The work he had been doing for the railroad testified to his competency and qualifications, and would in fact continue to do so because Twitchell continued to represent the A. T. & S. F. while serving as the district attorney. Today, an appointment such as this would have compelled Twitchell to leave the employ of the railway before assuming the DA's office, but in the nineteenth century there was apparently very little trepidation or concern over such conflicts of interest. Therefore, Twitchell was able to maintain both positions simultaneously. In fact, he actually carried out the duties of three influential posts at the same time. As the district attorney for Santa Fe County, Twitchell was also charged with executing the duties of the Solicitor General's office as well.

Early in 1889, the New Mexico Legislative Assembly created the office of Solicitor General. The new position, however, was designated to be held in abeyance and unoccupied until October of the same year. In the interim, the powers and duties of the office were to be discharged by the District Attorney of Santa Fe County, which meant that for most of that year, R. E. Twitchell was the acting Solicitor General for the territory.[91] He was juggling responsibilities to the A. T. & S. F. Railroad, New Mexico's First Judicial District, and the territorial government all at once, not to mention his growing familial obligations. Twitchell was certainly busy, stretched thin even, but that was what he had always wanted. He was finally vested with civic responsibilities. There was a problem, however, one that would devolve into an ugly feud between Twitchell and a fellow attorney named Jacob Crist.

Despite the territorial legislature's intent to leave the office of Solicitor General vacant and inchoate for a period of time following its creation, lame duck Democratic Governor Edmund G. Ross attempted to fill the position by appointing one of his political disciples, Jacob Crist, before the inauguration of his successor. Trying to sneak the appointment through before it could be challenged, Ross filled the Solicitor General's post, along with several others, while the legislative council was in recess, all of which was prohibited by law. The governor's power to make territorial appointments with the legislature in recess was limited to occurrences of death and resignation only.[92]

The shady contrivance was a desperate attempt by the Democratic Party to maintain some level of control over territorial governance as New Mexico transitioned into Republican hands. Believing that the commissioned officer would possess an unassailable claim to the position, Ross moved to install a Democrat using what he determined to be a loophole in the legislation that had created the office. As Ross and the Democrats saw the situation, regardless of legislative intent, the Solicitor General's office had been officially brought into existence during Governor Ross' tenure, and it was the sitting governor's prerogative to hand out appointments within the territorial government. Ross was merely exercising his gubernatorial privilege.[93] It was underhanded, but the prospective benefits far outweighed the potential costs. If the scheme held up, the Democrats would secure several important appointments within the territorial judiciary that otherwise were likely to be filled by Republicans. Conversely, if the plot were unsuccessful Ross and his colluders stood to lose nothing. Besides, there was a high likelihood of success. Once installed, the appointees would hold prima facie title to the offices, which would be extremely difficult to contest and likely to be upheld in court. Common law precedents in proceedings of this kind tended to favor the newly installed appointees over anyone contesting their right and title to the office.[94]

Ross and the Democrats appeared to have circumvented the legislature. It was a major coup, or at least it would have been if not for the fact that when Crist asserted his claim to the office, Twitchell ignored him and continued to exercise the duties of the Solicitor General. Crist then demanded that he desist, and Twitchell flatly refused. He had no intention of allowing a devious political maneuver to undermine the new administration. Twitchell candidly rejected Crist's commission as invalid. Spurned by the brash district attorney, Crist filed a lawsuit against him, asserting that he was entitled to the office by gubernatorial appointment, and that Twitchell was unlawfully performing the job of the Solicitor General without the authority to do so.[95]

As the ensuing courtroom drama unfolded, Crist was confident that the courts would find in his favor. With a commission from the former governor, he had a clearer title to the office than did Twitchell, who as DA was merely charged with executing the duties of the office until it was filled. If common law practices prevailed, Twitchell would be forced to relinquish the office, and Crist would be confirmed to that post. However, the presiding judge ruled that the legislature had not created the office of Solicitor General in presenti, but had merely declared that the office would come into existence at a later time. Therefore, no one could possess right and title to an office that did not yet exist. Crist's petition was denied, and the costs of the proceeding were charged against him.[96]a Confirmed as acting Solicitor General, Twitchell continued in that capacity until October 1889, at which point Governor Prince appointed Republican lawyer Edward Bartlett to the position.[96]b The decision rendered against Crist in his unsuccessful bid for the solicitor generalship meant that the other appointments made by Governor Ross during his last days in office were also liable to be ruled unconstitutional and invalid.

The New Mexico Democrats' political ploy had failed. For his part, Jacob Crist had suffered the public humiliation of having his gubernatorial appointment denied, and was made to appear foolishly ignorant of the territory's laws, in addition to having been saddled with the court costs. Angered by the outcome and feeling swindled, Crist began a newspaper he called The Santa Fe Sun and utilized it to voice his frustration.[97] From this platform he waged a propaganda campaign against New Mexico Republicans in general, and R. E. Twitchell in particular. Apparently, Crist personally identified Twitchell with the perceived affront that he had recently endured in court. Bent on vengeance, he began hounding Twitchell relentlessly. Throughout 1890 and 1891, torrents of vitriolic criticism aimed at the county prosecutor regularly appeared in The Sun. Any judicial missteps by the DA became fodder for the front page. Nor was Crist above distorting picayune events into propaganda to vilify Twitchell.

Slanderous journalism of this kind had become an accepted practice well before the 1890s, and like many others, Crist was taking full advantage of his resources. The dynamic between Republicans and Democrats in New Mexico had grown particularly ugly by this time, and both parties had taken to bashing the opposition in print. Each side published distortions and even total fabrications in an effort to subvert the other's influence within the territory. As the two factions upbraided and denigrated each other in the newspapers, character assassinations became more frequent. This hostile atmosphere of political persecution led to a lot of anger and suspicion among New Mexicans and to occasional eruptions of brutality and violence between Republicans and Democrats. In a few extreme instances, it even provoked murders. Having been charged with prosecuting crimes in Santa Fe, Rio Arriba, and San Juan counties, Twitchell was at the epicenter of this firestorm. When Republicans and Democrats transgressed against each other, it fell to him to prosecute each of the cases objectively. Searching out pretexts to attack Twitchell, Crist and the Democratic press subjected his performance as DA to intense scrutiny, and the indictments he secured against Democrats regularly generated accusations of partiality and bias. A personal vendetta may have made Twitchell the focus of Crist's wrath, but it was Twitchell's cachet as a high profile Republican that really made him a target for the opposition press.

Relations between Democrats and Republicans were particularly disputatious within the territorial capital where members of both parties worked and resided. In Santa Fe, political opponents interacted on a regular basis though rarely in accord. They squabbled in the territorial legislature, sneered at one another in the streets, and eyeballed each other in the cathedrals and churches. Intrigue bred mistrust and contributed to the lack of rapport. There was also the ever-present specter of bribery and corruption contaminating political interactions. In short, the community was sharply divided. Festivities, social gatherings and city functions attended by both factions were permeated by an uncomfortable awkwardness. On most of these occasions a tense civility reigned, but there was always the possibility altercations could break out, truncating the revelry with an exchange of gunfire.

Violence of this nature tended to breed reprisals, particularly in cases where the perpetrator managed to avoid prosecution under the law. When the legal system failed to satisfy the vengeful compatriots of homicide victims, further bloodshed was almost assured. To avenge their fallen brethren, normally law-abiding citizens embraced vigilantism and morphed into criminals with frightening ease. A seemingly isolated altercation could trigger a chain of retributive murders, transforming the capital city into a shooting gallery ruled by the precepts of talion. This cycle of brutality kept district attorney Twitchell exceedingly busy. Unfortunately, it also made him eminently assailable in the press.

When Twitchell brought an indictment against Santa Fe County Sheriff Francisco Chavez in 1890, for bludgeoning a murder suspect being held in the county jail, The Santa Fe Sun leapt to accuse the DA of political persecution. Sheriff Chavez was one of New Mexico's leading Democrats, and the prisoner,

Francisco Gonzales y Borrego, was a Democrat turned Republican. Complicating matters further, the man that Borrego was alleged to have killed, Jose Silvestre Gallegos, was also a popular Santa Fe Democrat. These sectarian circumstances provided Jacob Crist and his newspaper with an opportunity to attack the motives of the district attorney. When Chavez was arrested and arraigned on the charge of assault with a deadly weapon, The Sun insinuated that Twitchell had procured the indictment exclusively for the purpose of defaming a political adversary. In a scathing editorial Crist asserted that Twitchell's actions concealed underlying partisan objectives, and that the charges against Chavez were little more than a shameful and clumsy attempt to railroad a celebrated public servant. After the case was heard by a judge, the principal charge against Chavez was dismissed, and the sheriff agreed to plead guilty to assault and battery. Despite the fact that Twitchell secured a conviction in the case, Crist cast the judge's ruling as a complete repudiation of the indictment against Chavez. Triumphantly, The Sun announced that Twitchell's efforts to destroy Chavez had actually resulted in a tremendous boost to the sheriff's popularity.[98]

The bloody partisan warfare plaguing the capital continued, and as the district attorney for Santa Fe County, Twitchell was right in the middle of the melee. Since the warring factions were almost constantly in the courts, Twitchell prosecuted both Borrego and Chavez on different occasions. He failed to get either of them locked away in the penitentiary, however, and as a result the row between these men ended up playing out on the streets of Santa Fe.

Not long after the Gallegos slaying, another body was discovered in an arroyo south of the city that appeared to be linked to the Chavez-Borrego feud. The corpse was that of Faustin Ortiz, a Republican ward politician and a witness for the defense in the forthcoming murder case against Borrego. He had been summarily executed and buried in a shallow grave. The exhaustive investigation that followed yielded evidence implicating several local peace officers in the crime, men connected to Santa Fe County Sheriff Francisco Chavez.[99]

District Attorney Twitchell was again faced with trying to secure an indictment against this renowned public figure. The prospect of this probably excited him, considering that Chavez had sidestepped his previous prosecution attempt. Taking another run at the sheriff would of course mean suffering more abuse in the pages of The Sun, but the bad publicity would amount to very little if Twitchell could secure a conviction against Chavez for the serious crime of which he now stood accused. Should Twitchell succeed in linking the county sheriff to the assassination of a witness in a murder trial, Crist's pronouncements of ruinous intent would appear disreputable, and the DA would be vindicated publicly. At the very least Twitchell wanted to see Chavez locked up for abusing his powers as sheriff and violating New Mexico's laws. Under no illusions as to the difficulties facing him, Twitchell set to work building another case against the sheriff and his toadies.

In truth, there very well may have been a hidden Republican agenda to ruin Sheriff Chavez, just as Jacob Crist repeatedly charged in his newspaper. In 1890, Thomas Catron's Republican League was embroiled in a violent struggle against the Democratic machine headed by Romulo Martinez and Francisco Chavez.[100] Therefore, it is possible that the local Republican elite would conspire against the sheriff. There was certainly no warmth between Twitchell and Chavez, and given Twitchell's political affiliation with Catron, the Republican headman, it's very possible that the two colluded in an effort to destroy Chavez and any number of other New Mexico Democrats. However, without concrete evidence corroborating Crist's assertions in The Sun, it is difficult to determine whether Twitchell's indictments of Francisco Chavez should be construed as politically motivated aggression, or the mere dispensation of justice, or a combination of the two. Regardless of any political plotting that may or may not have been going on, the cases brought against Chavez were not unfounded. The sheriff was apparently operating outside the law, which made it possible for Twitchell, perhaps encouraged by shadowy Republican officials, to call his conduct into question.

Compiling the evidence in the Ortiz murder took Twitchell and his colleagues months to complete. They chased down even the most improbable leads, and interrogated numerous suspects, but the case they built against Chavez and his accomplices was far from airtight. Should the case make it to trial, the outcome was anything but assured. In no hurry to face the withering criticisms of Crist and his associates, Twitchell held off submitting indictments in the case until the last moment. Finally on the second to last day of the August 1890 term of the district court for Santa Fe County, the DA's office filed indictments against sixteen co-conspirators for complicity in the Ortiz killing. Among them was Sheriff Frank Chavez, Twitchell's main quarry. The prosecution had assembled twenty witnesses willing to testify against the group, and appeared ready to roll the dice, but the trial would have to wait until the courts reconvened.[101]

As before, Jacob Crist hovered around the proceedings, looking for reasons to berate the DA. With each new development in the case, The Sun printed editorials castigating Twitchell's dispensation of the matter. When Twitchell launched a probe into some rumors circulating about the murder victim's missing handgun, Crist made the inquiry out to be a witch-hunt. He asserted that the story had been concocted by the territory's Republican contingent for wholly partisan purposes, and even went so far as to print notarized affidavits filled with claims of coercion to substantiate his speculations.[102]

Throughout the August 1890 term of the Santa Fe County District Court, while Twitchell was preparing his case against Chavez, The Santa Fe Sun unapologetically ran editorials denouncing him as a venal scoundrel. Moreover, the vengeful Democrat editor broadened his attack, charging Twitchell with squandering the fiscal appropriation for territorial grand jury witness fees and using territorial funds to pay Republicans for party services.[103] The newspaper repeatedly devoted its front page to publicizing this imagined arrangement in which the diabolical district attorney paid Republicans with public monies to testify in court cases in which they had no involvement. Twitchell attempted to answer Crist's charges in the editorial columns of The New Mexican, a rival paper with Republican sympathies, but his response just provided Crist with more fuel for his vendetta. In his explanation Twitchell attributed the profuse outlay of funds and the glut of witnesses, to the exhaustive investigation of the Ortiz murder. In response Crist unleashed a sarcastic vituperation denouncing the justification as a complete falsehood, and Twitchell as a profligate liar.[104] Over successive weeks The Sun's attacks grew even more virulent. Twitchell was accused of carrying a concealed weapon in violation of the gun law, of failing to prosecute Republican lawbreakers, and of stacking the current Santa Fe county grand and petit juries with Republican peons.[105]

By the time R. E. Twitchell actually filed indictments against Chavez and his lackeys, Crist's campaign against him was in full swing. In response to the filing, the editor of The Sun alleged that Twitchell had deliberately withheld the indictments until the penultimate day of the term to guarantee that the trial could not take place until the courts reconvened.[106] This meant that the case would remain unresolved through the territorial elections in November of that year. More importantly, the delay meant that Twitchell, a candidate for a seat in the territorial assembly, did not have to risk an embarrassing courtroom defeat prior to the election.[107] The indictment of the sheriff for murder made Twitchell appear to be an intrepid crusader for justice, at least to some, and provided him with first-rate electioneering material. For Crist, Twitchell's delay of the indictments was proof of a Republican conspiracy. He decried the indictments against the sheriff and his men as fallacious, and implied that they were designed to make Twitchell appear highly efficacious before the forthcoming elections.[108] As he saw it, the move was a disgraceful attempt by the DA to use his current office for political gain, and nothing more than a ruse to deceive voters. Allusions to a sinister plot designed to pack the territorial bureaucracy with Republican flunkies appeared in the pages of The Sun to support the charge. According to Crist, New Mexico Republicans were looking to force an exploitative state constitution through the territorial legislature in a shameful attempt to benefit personally from the transition to statehood.[109] Accomplishing this required garnering popular support, which he suggested, Republicans were unabashedly pursuing by means of bribery, misinformation, and coercion. At the heart of the conspiracy Crist placed Twitchell, along with "Boss" Thomas Catron.

As the election approached, Crist kept up his barrage against Twitchell, even after the latter withdrew as a candidate for representative from Santa Fe County to concentrate on the impending Chavez case.[110] In September, an admonition concerning the future dispensation of that particular case appeared in The Sun, warning Twitchell that he need fear legal reprisals if the charges proved erroneous.[111] Still, with no new developments in the case, the paper had little fodder. Crist had to settle for rehashing the assertion that Twitchell was part of a Republican plot to manipulate prospective voters in the upcoming election. The indignant editor was simply determined to see Twitchell suffer the agony of humiliation. A week before the election, Crist called Twitchell an unworthy and unpatriotic officer, and asserted that he had openly boasted that the Republicans would buy the votes they needed in Santa Fe County.[112]

If there was indeed a Republican conspiracy to affect the outcome of the election, it apparently was successful. After the results were tabulated, Republican Thomas Catron won the Santa Fe County seat in the legislative assembly.[113] With the political race over and the courts in recess until the following year, Crist could have relented, but he continued to harass Twitchell as opportunities arose. When Twitchell's commission as DA was winding up at the end of the year and his re-nomination appeared to be in question, Crist printed an editorial mocking him.[114] The editor's schadenfreude, however, was premature; the rumors regarding Twitchell being dislodged from the district attorney's office were untrue. Governor Prince had every intention of reappointing Twitchell as the prosecutor for the first judicial district. In January 1891, the legislative council unanimously confirmed Twitchell's nomination, retaining him for another two-year term.[115]

R. E. Twitchell initiated his second term in the DA's office with the much anticipated prosecution of Francisco Chavez and his cohorts in February 1891. Surprisingly, Jacob Crist, the nearly perpetual thorn in Twitchell's side over the preceding months, printed very little as the case got underway. The Sun's editor had apparently lost some of the ill will he had previously harbored for Twitchell.

Though the media spotlight had faded somewhat, the Faustin Ortiz murder trial still attracted public attention. Interest remained high because convictions in the case would deal a crippling blow to one of New Mexico's most powerful Democratic machines. Additionally, the trial featured a veritable who's who of Santa Fe citizenry. Besides several high profile defendants and the illustrious district attorney, Twitchell's friend and mentor Henry Waldo represented Francisco Chavez and at least one other defendant.[116] Highly respected Judge Edward P. Seeds presided.

The proceedings ran through the middle of the month and were extremely contentious, ultimately turning on a technicality. The determining factor proved to be pleas of abatement filed by the defendants that called into question the constitutionality of the territory's jury law. "Several points were raised, but the principal one was that the grand jury that indicted [the defendants] was not a jury of the vicinage," and therefore violated the constitutional rights of the defendants.[117] At the time, Santa Fe County district court terms were held concurrently with terms of the first judicial district court of the United States, in the courthouse at Santa Fe. To fill their grand and petit juries, both courts utilized the same pool of jurors made up of men from throughout the first judicial district, which consisted of Santa Fe, Rio Arriba, and San Juan counties. The defense argued that since six members of the grand jury that brought the indictments resided outside of Santa Fe County they were technically not from the "vicinage" in a Santa Fe County court case.[118] Therefore, these jurors could not lawfully be used to adjudicate Santa Fe County cases. Twitchell, and his co-counsel, Solicitor General Bartlett, rebutted the claim, stating that the Grand Jury was "legal and regular and lawful," so the indictments should stand.[119] The prosecution's arguments were compelling;

"testimony in some of the cases [being] very strong, and ... [leaving] no doubt but that the indictments were found upon full and convincing proof."[120] In the end, however, Judge Seeds declared the indictments illegal on the grounds that "the grand jury that found [them] was unconstitutional."[121] Chavez and the other defendants were free, for the moment anyway.

In response to the Judge's ruling that the indictments were illegal, Crist resumed his campaign against Twitchell with another round of scathing editorials. While significantly less pointed than his previous denunciations, this series of attacks was a rehashing of the accusation that the district attorney had brought the indictments against Chavez and the other Democrats for purely partisan reasons. Included in the editorial was a demand that Twitchell try the case again as soon as possible. The Sun's editor charged that allowing the case to rest, having been decided on a technicality failed to satisfy the DA's "obligations under [the] oath of office ... as well as [the defendants'] sacred right of vindication."[122] A murder charge could not be so easily swept under the carpet and forgotten, asserted Crist.

An immediate retrial, however, was impossible. The judge's finding that the jury law was unconstitutional had "brought all territorial business to a standstill."[123] A new jury law had to be passed by the legislature before proceedings could resume. To the relief of all New Mexicans, a new law was expeditiously pushed through the legislature, and the courts quickly resumed functioning. By August 1891, nearly a year after the indictments against Chavez and the others had originally been filed, the Faustin Ortiz murder trial was again being adjudicated in a New Mexico courtroom. However, the trial had been removed south to Albuquerque, and presumably to the consternation of Jacob Crist, the prosecuting officer was no longer Ralph Twitchell. The change of venue put Thomas Catron in charge of the case instead; while Neill B. Field, a prominent Democrat, took over for the defense. The location may have shifted, but the result was similar to before. Francisco Chavez and his co-defendants were once again acquitted on a technicality.[124]

The sheriff and the other suspects were exonerated, but the moment was disappointing for Jacob Crist. Twitchell's dissociation from the case prevented the spiteful editor from reveling in the outcome. Not only that, after the suspects that Twitchell had assembled were reindicted, any questions about the validity of the original indictments or the DA's motivations were moot. The charges of blatant partisanship and malfeasance leveled by Crist over so many months were revealed to be baseless, politically motivated propaganda. Twitchell was publicly vindicated. Rather than a bigoted persecutor of Democrats, he was recast in the public forum as a persecuted champion of justice. True or not, this revelation repaired any damage that had been inflicted upon Twitchell's credibility as the district attorney. Crist's campaign had failed to tear him down. What's more, Crist had been humiliated once again, having been exposed as a libelous, partisan scandalmonger.

R. E. Twitchell waded through the remainder of his second term in the DA's office without having to endure more abuse from Jacob Crist. Given the public thrashing that Crist's credibility had suffered, and that Twitchell was in the process of acquiring "a reputation second to none in the territory as a prosecuting officer," it would have been difficult for the embittered editor to continue his venomous crusade.[125] The Santa Fe Sun, Crist's paper, continued to cover the area's court proceedings and in doing so regularly printed Twitchell's name, but its editorials were noticeably devoid of contemptuous rhetoric. Twitchell no longer had to contend with an almost constant stream of denigration and was finally able to exercise the duties of his office without having to defend his motives every step of the way. Even indictments brought against Democrats did not incite further vitriol from Crist, who appeared to be rethinking his hostility for the DA.

Though Jacob Crist's attempts to vilify Twitchell abated, the politically motivated violence that was contextual to the editor's erstwhile propaganda campaign remained a pressing issue in Santa Fe. The combative partisanship that had sparked the slaying of Silvestre Gallegos, and provided the impetus for the Faustin Ortiz killing had not diminished. Shrouded in the anonymity of secret societies, Republicans and Democrats continued to exchange gunfire in the capital city. The quarrel between Chavez and Borrego continued to deteriorate over several years until both men wound up dead, along with at least six of their associates "in the most intense and horrible chain of murders, assassinations, and conspiracies ever concocted within the borders of New Mexico."[126] On May 29, 1892, unknown assailants shot and killed Francisco Chavez, the former sheriff who had repeatedly eluded territorial prosecutors. Four days later, Chavez's friend Juan Pablo Dominguez was also gunned down. Implicated in both shootings was none other than Francisco y Borrego, the same man who had killed Gallegos two years earlier. There was little doubt that all these shootings were linked, the casualties of a politically inspired gang war. [127]

The anarchic situation in Santa Fe constituted a total breakdown of the democratic system, which consequently caught the attention of the national government. The string of politically motivated murders ultimately prompted newly elected Democratic President Grover Cleveland to appoint William T. Thornton as governor of the territory in May 1893. A former mayor of Santa Fe, Thornton was selected because of his familiarity with the circumstances, and charged with curtailing the bloodshed plaguing the territorial capital. The new governor immediately set up a task force to address the violence and restore order in Santa Fe. This detail successfully reduced the murderous political intrigue within the capital. They were even able to bring some closure to the whole sordid episode by arresting, convicting, and hanging four men for the Chavez killing, including that prolific slayer of Democrats, Francisco y Borrego.[128]

In the course of cleaning up Santa Fe, Governor Thornton replaced a number of the territory's judicial officials. Among those discharged was District Attorney R. E. Twitchell. While some of the unseated individuals may have been ousted for legitimate reasons, the removal of Twitchell carried ominous partisan overtones. Twitchell was singled out within days of the new regime's takeover and expelled from the DA's office on a flimsy, trumped-up charge. On May 26, 1893 Twitchell received a letter from Governor Thornton notifying him that his commission as district attorney would be revoked. The Governor explained that he had received information, which he believed to be reliable, that made Twitchell ineligible to hold the position. According to an unnamed source, Twitchell was indebted to the territory, as well as to the counties of Santa Fe, Rio Arriba, and San Juan, for large sums of money. This debt disqualified Twitchell from being eligible to hold the post to which he had been appointed. Responding to the charge, Twitchell explained that he was not, under any circumstances, in debt to the territory or any of the counties therein. He also stated that he was both willing and able to prove his innocence in the matter. This, however, appears to have been beside the issue; Twitchell's guilt or innocence seems to have had no bearing on the governor's decision to replace him.[129]

Governor Thornton's actions concerning R. E. Twitchell reeked of partisan machination and personal vendetta. There was no valid reason for removing him from office; he had actually been one of the few people "taking measures to stop the lawlessness and carrying of six shooters," within Santa Fe.[130] Yet, despite being an exceedingly proficient trial lawyer with no definite ties to the gang war on the street other than his Republican affiliation, or his role as prosecutor of the combatants, Twitchell was still ignominiously dismissed. Far from a victim of the standard procedure accompanying a change of administration, Twitchell was removed for cause with his term in office about to expire. His inclusion in the political purge, while framed as executive prerogative, actually appears to have been a thinly veiled attempt to diminish his stature within the community. Not only was Twitchell unceremoniously expelled from office in the waning months of his four-year tenure for supposedly being ineligible to hold public office according to the provisions of a legislative act that had been brought into existence just five months earlier.[131] But also, in his place the governor appointed none other than Jacob Crist, Twitchell's former persecutor, and presumably an accomplice in this latest plot against him, perhaps even the unnamed accuser.[132] Far from coincidental, the Governor's supplanting of Twitchell with Crist had been a deliberate act meant to clearly communicate to the besieged DA exactly why he was being removed from office. Crist was quite obviously a Democratic crony of Thornton's, and once the latter became governor, Crist found himself in a position to secure his revenge against Twitchell. These circumstances give every indication that Twitchell was out, one-way or another, his political career and professional reputation potentially compromised by Jacob Crist's pettiness.

With Governor Thornton serving as avenger, Jacob Crist finally succeeded in his mission to debase Ralph Twitchell. It took the better part of four years and the ascension of a Democratic governor amenable to his desire for revenge, but Crist managed to make Twitchell look bad. As for R. E. Twitchell, he had had enough. The lengthy assault from Crist; all the abuse he had endured, convinced him "that office holding was a thankless business," and he wanted no part of it going forward. To the disappointment of Republicans throughout the territory who saw him as one of the most efficacious members of their party, Twitchell decided that he would never again be a candidate for any public office.[133]

5

May(or), May Not

"I was the youngest mayor of the oldest city in the United States"
—Ralph Emerson Twitchell[134]

After four long years in the district attorney's office R. E. Twitchell was disillusioned by his experiences as a civil servant. The episode with Jacob Crist had altered his perception of partisan politics and driven him to discard his political aspirations. He had no intention of placing himself in a similar situation again; the aggravation that arose conjunctively was simply intolerable. Twitchell meant to continue his work for the Republican Party, campaigning for candidates and promulgating the ideology, but he had abandoned the idea of a career in politics. The denizens of Santa Fe, however, had plans of their own for the jaded district attorney.

Many Santa Feans, both Democrat and Republican, fretted over Twitchell's decision to abstain from politics, believing he was one of New Mexico's most competent statesmen. A group of concerned citizens even beseeched Twitchell to reconsider, and persisted in attempts to revive his interest in holding office. In 1893, Santa Fe was beginning to modernize and these intuitive individuals undoubtedly understood that a progressive, civic-minded legal virtuoso like Twitchell would be incredibly valuable as the city transitioned from an outmoded commercial hub to a modern metropolis. Unwilling to be denied, Santa Fe's citizens continued to solicit Twitchell's help despite his refusals.

Disenchanted with politics, Ralph Twitchell was unabashed about expressing his distaste with the way civic affairs were conducted in New Mexico. He even went as far as to broadcast his cynicism through a local journalist when he made his pronouncement that he was finished with public office. Word of Twitchell's decision spread quickly as the region's newspapers reprinted his comments. In Santa Fe, many residents received the news with surprise and skepticism, because prior to the announcement Twitchell had appeared destined for a long career as a civil servant. Less than two years before, The Santa Fe Daily New Mexican had proclaimed that "in the entire territory there probably is no young man so well equipped and posted in public affairs" as Ralph Twitchell.[135] That he would throw away a promising political career in protest of the status quo, simply strained credulity. Therefore, his colleagues perceived Twitchell's untimely withdrawal from politics as more of a sabbatical than an outright exit.

When it became clear to all concerned that Twitchell was indeed finished as an office-seeker, a ripple of anxiety ran through New Mexico Republicans, and a few Democrats for that matter. Twitchell was one of the most adroit statesmen in the entire territory; his abstention from public service was a loss not only for the Republican Party but for the territorial bureaucracy as well. Recognizing this, a group of Santa Fe citizens approached Twitchell about reconsidering. While conferring with Twitchell the assemblage floated the idea that he would make a fine mayor, and asked if he could be persuaded to run in the upcoming 1893 election. Reluctant to reimmerse himself in the political morass, Twitchell demurred, citing "pressing official and private business interests."[136]

R. E. Twitchell's refusal to stand for the mayoralty of Santa Fe should have brought the matter to a close, but the contingent of citizens desirous of seeing him continue in politics was not easily dissuaded. In the month preceding the April 1893 Santa Fe city elections, a petition appeared in a local newspaper imploring Twitchell to permit the submission of his name as a candidate for mayor. The entreaty stated, "that the time [had] come [for] new and active blood [to] be infused into the city government," and expressed confidence in Twitchell as someone who would "spare no effort to make the city progressive and modern in every way possible." Included in the list of names were members of both political parties and many of Santa Fe's most respected residents.[137]

As complimentary as the appeal was, blandishments failed to entice R. E. Twitchell into becoming a mayoral candidate. As before, Twitchell declined, and again his refusal did nothing to discourage his supporters, who still had one more card to play. On the night of March 25, 1893 the Republican delegates to the city convention assembled at the courthouse to decide on the party ticket. When nominations were in order, delegate Marcos Castillo presented Ralph Twitchell's name for mayor, and the congregation erupted in a thunderous ovation. Amid the applause Twitchell was nominated by acclamation. Though Twitchell maintained that he was not interested in the position, five days later the Santa Fe Weekly New Mexican Review printed the Republican city ticket with his name prominently displayed as the mayoral nominee. Included in the article was a paragraph supporting his candidacy. It described him as "full of energy and enterprise," and proclaimed that electing him "even against his wishes ... would be a progressive step for the capital city." Despite his repeated objections, Twitchell was once again a candidate for public office.[138]

Even after being forced into the mayoral race, Twitchell remained apathetic. He appears to have done no campaigning of any kind. Nevertheless, when the votes were tabulated, R. E. Twitchell had been chosen as mayor of Santa Fe.[139]

The "youngest mayor of the oldest city," Ralph Emerson Twitchell.
Sketch from the Santa Fe New Mexican, September 9, 1891

The city's inhabitants selected Twitchell against his wishes because they recognized him as one of the most progressive citizens in the entire territory and believed his insight and guidance would be invaluable in the days ahead. Santa Fe was at a crossroads in the early 1890s. The once great terminal of Southwestern commerce was suffering from an identity crisis. The Santa Fe Trail, formerly the most significant shipping route in the region, had ceased to have importance since the arrival of the railroad. This drop-off transformed the city from a bustling commercial center into an economic backwater almost overnight. Faced with the possibility that Santa Fe could become a ghost town, the citizenry undertook modernizing measures to save their city. Their first order of business was undergoing incorporation, which they succeeded in doing in 1891.[140] Two years later when Twitchell was elected mayor, city officials were still laying out the code of laws and constructing the utility infrastructure. There remained a great deal to accomplish, and skilled politicians were needed to expedite the process because the threat of fading into obscurity was very real. Other New Mexico towns, Albuquerque in particular, were attempting to supplant Santa Fe as the territorial capital.[141] This would be the final nail in Santa Fe's coffin dooming the already languishing city to irrelevancy and ultimately consigning it to the past. Fearful of being swept aside, Santa Fe residents were scrambling to "be up and doing on progressive lines," believing that it was their only hope of retaining the capital.[142] Consequently, they sought the leadership of forward thinking individuals like R. E. Twitchell, whether they liked it or not.

Electing Twitchell to the mayor's office in this turbulent time was effectively a vote of confidence from Santa Feans. The residents of the territorial capital were calling on him to do his civic duty. An opportunity to fulfill his assumed familial obligation to develop the nation was laid out before him. How could he refuse? Left with little choice in the matter, Twitchell finally consented to serve as mayor of Santa Fe.

Once in the mayor's office Twitchell hit the ground running. First, "a great deal of routine business necessary upon a change of administration was given attention."[143a] Then Twitchell and the rest of the city council set to work, endeavoring to continue the modernization of Santa Fe without delay. Picking up right where his predecessors William Taylor Thornton and Manuel Valdes had left off, Twitchell carried on the innovative efforts to bring the city up to date that had started two years earlier. Even before Twitchell's mayoral appointments had been confirmed, he and the council were dealing with the U.S. Treasury department, arranging to have sidewalks laid around the federal building.[143]b

Other projects similarly aimed at developing the town followed. Twitchell's tenure in office capped off a period of tremendously productive growth in Santa Fe. From 1891 to 1893, the municipal government enacted a variety of new ordinances, most of which were related to the city's infrastructure and the quality of life of its citizens. Concentrating on making Santa Fe habitable, Twitchell and the other city administrators introduced new amenities such as an underground sewer system and electric lighting. Additionally, "The construction, operation, and maintenance of a water supply system to fulfill domestic and public purposes received considerable attention."[144]a Provisions were made for creating a reservoir, and for laying pipes and placing hydrants about town. This was a massive multi-year undertaking that included sorting out issues of water rights and balancing the needs of the municipality and its rural surroundings.[144]b

Twitchell's term in office also coincided with the establishment of the city's governing ordinances. Prior to 1891, there were few laws in Santa Fe pertaining to the personal conduct and behavior of residents. Twitchell and the other city council members in office during the early 1890s were in the position of having to define the regulatory guidelines of their community. This meant confronting everything from heath concerns, to public safety issues, to a multitude of pernicious behaviors. Public intoxication and indecent exposure were both prohibited, as were fireworks and the discharging of firearms. Disturbing the peace, disrupting religious services, and racing horses through the city's thoroughfares were all defined as illicit activities as well. Likewise, prostitution and opium use were addressed as nuisances. During this extraordinarily busy time for the city government, there was a conspicuous effort to make Santa Fe more cosmopolitan.[145]

At that time Santa Fe still retained much of its original bucolic character, so many of the new regulations dealt with controlling animals. "Cattle, horses, mules, burros, goats, sheep, and swine received specific enumeration as species that could not run at large within the city limits."[146]a Additionally, prospective health hazards, such as those relating to the proper disposal of animal carcasses were addressed. All told, the list of statutes and regulations published in 1893 filled more than a hundred pages.[146]b

A portion of the revamping measures implemented by city government impinged upon the ways in which many Santa Fean's worked and lived. Not surprisingly, some residents balked at these changes. Complaints and objections regularly arose as the new ordinances inconvenienced people and upset established subsistence methods. The increased taxes that were intended to help offset the cost of bringing Santa Fe up to date frustrated the city's poorer inhabitants, who did not suffer in silence. Numerous residents were also critical of the law passed against shooting fowl in one's own backyard. Complicating the situation, several of the freshly empowered city agencies failed to perform their duties adequately. Garbage collection and street cleaning were two areas that were particularly deficient, and the cause of a fair amount of discontent within the populace.[147]

Comprehending that the daunting and amorphous task of urbanizing Santa Fe would ultimately require assistance from the general public, Twitchell reached out to his constituency. In an attempt to inform the public of the city's requirements and coerce cooperation in their fulfillment, he wrote a "readable letter" to the citizens of Santa Fe "on the subject of needed improvements to the city."[148a] He then submitted the missive to The Santa Fe New Mexican for publication.[148b]

Though Twitchell harbored misgivings about the effectiveness of newspapers at disseminating information, he felt compelled to publish the list of imperative ameliorations because he appreciated the necessity of overhauling the city's infrastructure. His somewhat disdainful opinion of the press stemmed from a belief that newspapers accomplished very little in New Mexico, because only a small portion of the population could read.[149] Conscious of the fact that he was appealing to a limited number of educated professionals; Twitchell was counting on the city's intelligentsia to pass the message along to their uneducated associates. Listing the needed civic improvements in the newspaper was a less than reliable means of amassing support for the initiative, but with few other options, Twitchell was forced to reconcile the medium's shortcomings with the reality of the situation. He needed support from the community if he was going to succeed in polishing Santa Fe into the jewel he envisioned it to be.

Twitchell's doubts notwithstanding, the article seems to have had its intended effect. The enterprising exploits of Ralph Twitchell and his fellow city administrators during this transformative stage in Santa Fe's development were largely successful. Their efforts were so thorough that the legal precepts they established remained virtually unchanged well into the twentieth century, at which point new technologies forced alterations to be made.[150] As a result, the city was slowly being transformed into a progressive urban center complete with modern conveniences. Still, the process was gradual, and the day-to-day existence of residents carried on much as it had before the reforms were instituted. Even with the changes to the city's law code, daily life in Santa Fe remained raucous and unpredictable. Sporadic outbreaks of violence continued to unnerve and agitate the community.

The publication of the "readable letter" made Twitchell an even more recognizable figure in Santa Fe politics. The editorial tied him, by name, to the improvements being outlined, undoubtedly raising the public's perception of his role in passing the new resolutions. It reaffirmed his status as a man of the people, demonstrating his insightfulness and willingness to collaborate with others in order to accomplish a goal. Ultimately, Twitchell's appeal to Santa Feans' sense of civic responsibility enhanced his credibility as a public figure.

Though his duties as mayor did not extend as far as keeping the peace in Santa Fe, Twitchell took it upon himself to be actively involved in the administration of justice. When violence bloodied the capital's streets and a posse was needed to round up dangerous men, he was readily available, gun in hand.[151] More than just a politician, Ralph Twitchell was an agent of change, a luminary who literally led from the front and was willing to put himself in harms way to ensure that the modernization of Santa Fe continued unabated.

R. E. Twitchell's willingness to go above and beyond the mayoral job description to promote growth and cultivate civility in Santa Fe made him a local household name. Presiding over Santa Fe also provided him with bona fide political credentials. His role in establishing the city's laws and its utility reticule made him one of the leading patrons of Santa Fe's modern incarnation, as well as one of New Mexico's most prominent Republicans. In just a matter of months, Twitchell had become a standard-bearer for progress in the Southwest, and New Mexicans had come to see him as a bellwether. Any lingering questions about Twitchell's competence, his integrity, or his intentions that may have been raised during Jacob Crist's multi-year crusade against him had been dispelled resoundingly.

When Ralph Twitchell vacated the mayor's office in 1894, Santa Fe was well on its way to becoming a modern American city. Still, the future remained dubious and unpredictable. New Mexicans were embroiled in the fight for statehood. Santa Fe's land claim dispute with the federal government was still pending resolution. Albuquerque continued to harbor designs on becoming the capital, and intransigent political partisanship divided the territorial assembly. Further compounding matters, the country was mired in an economic downturn and divided over political issues such as free silver and the rights of labor and capital. There was no way to predict how everything would unfold in the coming years, but barring a catastrophe, Santa Fe was poised to thrive and retain its status as a commercial and political center.

R. E. Twitchell was just thirty-three years old when he was elected as Santa Fe's highest official. His youth and political inexperience notwithstanding, he had performed the duties of the office extremely well. Not only that, he had done it all pro bono, accepting no pay for his services throughout his tenure.[152] Seeing Santa Fe flourish was his priority, not lining his own pockets. He was not interested in advancing his political career either. When asked about his time in office, he would humbly downplay his significance, saying, "I was only mayor for about a year…I had 365 days of grief and I never tried the job again."[153] Twitchell remained an active participant in New Mexico politics long after he left the mayor's office, but true to his word he did not serve even one more day as an elected public official. Despite his personal renunciation of candidature, he managed to stay politically relevant for another quarter century by capitalizing on his skill as a public speaker and husting for New Mexico's Republican Party.

6
THE SILVER-TONGUED ORATOR of NEW MEXICO

"A great man is always willing to be little."
—Ralph Waldo Emerson

The mayoralty of Santa Fe was the last elected office that Ralph Twitchell ever held. When his term came to a close in 1894 he resumed abnegating political position; however, Twitchell's refusal to stand for public office was not an outright repudiation of politics. He continued to participate in the political arena, as an organizer, an appointee, and a campaigning kingmaker, for an additional fifteen years. His unwavering determination to refrain from further political candidacy had not nullified his commitment to civic affairs.

Having grown up in a family replete with American patriots, revolutionaries, pioneers, and governing officials, R. E. Twitchell could not, with a clear conscience, entirely abandon politics. His ancestors had helped forge the nation, had fostered its growth, and had served as agents of Americanization on its frontiers. Each successive generation was taught that civil service was an obligation of patriotism and inculcated with a strong sense of civic responsibility. As a result of this upbringing, R. E. Twitchell was devoted to the modernization and industrialization of the United States, and had an unquenchable desire to fulfill his perceived destiny as a pioneer and civilizer of America's frontier.

Like his father before him, Ralph Twitchell was a Republican. The party of Lincoln had managed to preserve the nation when insurrection threatened to destroy it, and in the years following the Civil War it had become an extremely powerful political entity. The GOP had been responsible for reconstructing the Union in the aftermath of the conflict and dominated national politics for the majority of Twitchell's youth. For a man as patriotic and ambitious as Twitchell, it was the logical choice. Once affiliated, he immersed himself completely in the party, giving freely of his time and money. Twitchell, however, was not so blinded by loyalty that he would readily compromise his principles in support of the party. In fact, he was unapologetically critical of Republicans that failed to live up to his expectations.[154]

From his earliest days in the territory Twitchell served as a promoter and campaigner for the GOP. His eloquence quickly made him an indispensable part of the Republican canvassing effort in New Mexico. An extremely forceful orator, he was capable of persuading entire crowds to vote Republican. Even before he had perfected his rhetorical style, Twitchell was regarded so highly as a lecturer that his mere presence at a political rally could incite calls from the throng entreating him to make an impromptu speech.[155]

By 1886, Ralph Twitchell had begun to climb the ranks of New Mexico's Republican Party. That year he was elected secretary of the Republican Territorial Central Committee and its Executive Committee. He continued in that capacity through 1888, and thus became embedded in the territory's political landscape. Thereafter, Twitchell began to be considered for appointments and positions in various governmental agencies and administrative bureaucracies within the territory. The following year he was appointed district attorney of New Mexico's first judicial district.[156]

Though his experiences as prosecutor ultimately made him weary of public service, his commitment to the Republican Party never wavered. During the four years that Twitchell served as DA, he also filled several other positions within the party's regional infrastructure. He was secretary of both the Santa Fe County Central Committee and the New Mexico Republican League, as well as the president of the fourth ward League Club of Santa Fe.[157]

Even after he resolved to forego public office beyond his tenure as DA, Twitchell remained dedicated to furthering the GOP and continued to hold posts within the party framework. In 1892, the same year he announced his decision to permanently forsake the pursuit of public office, he was elected chairman of the Republican Central Committee of New Mexico.[158] For more than three decades thereafter he served as a functionary, an organizer, and a mouthpiece for the party, and managed to maintain a significant presence in New Mexico politics. Twitchell traveled extensively throughout the region giving speeches and setting up Republican clubs and organizations.[159] He also campaigned on behalf of Republican candidates. His efforts in that regard led directly to the election of Republicans in Santa Fe County.[160]

Campaign stopovers and political rallies increased Twitchell's renown as an orator, and a growing public interest in his speeches prompted newspapers in the region to reprint some of the more rhapsodic portions of his addresses. Though Twitchell's message generally carried Republican overtones, his fluency, elocutionary style, and conspicuous concern for the welfare of New Mexico gave him mass appeal. Even area Democrats acknowledged his prowess as a speech-maker and on occasion enlisted him to speak before their assemblage. When Grover Cleveland was inaugurated President in 1893, New Mexico Democrats celebrated the victory with a party in the Santa Fe plaza. Revelers were treated to music and refreshments, as well as a few remarks from some of the territory's leading citizens. The evening's keynoter was Ralph Twitchell, who for his part was proud to address his fellow New Mexicans on such an auspicious occasion. Regardless of any political differences that may have divided them, they were all Americans. Not to mention that Twitchell had many friends in the Democratic Party. In fact, he was beloved despite the extended barrage of public criticism and attempts at character assassination that he had so recently endured at the hands of Jacob Crist. Far from a hostile crowd, those congregated that evening had begun to howl Twitchell's name while the band was still performing. After mounting the stage "amid the uproarious yells of the people," Twitchell delivered "one of his characteristic speeches."161a Perhaps with Jacob Crist in mind, he "declared that all men should rise above the level of partisan politics."161b He then stated that he considered "it an honor to address the people upon the ascendancy of any man to the loftiest official position in the world," and that even though "he was a Republican, dyed in the wool...Grover Cleveland was his president as well as the president of the Democrats."[161]c

Twitchell was undoubtedly conscious of his popularity and the possibilities for political advancement that a reputation like his own could provide, but he was dissatisfied with politics and uninterested in political advancement. While he enjoyed campaigning and the winning of elections, he no longer wanted to participate in the administration of government. Also, he recognized that in serving as a mouthpiece for the party he could promote innumerable nominees, and potentially help secure more political offices for Republicans than he could as a single self-promoting candidate. Since Twitchell desired to elevate his beloved Republican Party more than advance his own career, he devoted his extensive talents toward getting other members of his party elected to public offices.

In recognition of his contributions, R. E. Twitchell received countless commissions to serve as a delegate at a multitude of political conventions. He was also elected to a variety of positions within the Party, including a second and third term as the chairman of the Republican Territorial Central Committee in 1902 and 1903.[162] Twitchell's return to the chairmanship was no reverent gesture either; he was particularly effective in this capacity. Under his guidance the Republican Party scored the largest political victory in New Mexico history, up to that point.[163]

Regardless of the post he was filling, Twitchell was committed to expanding Republican influence, and therefore, generous with his time when it came to promoting the party platform. In addition to making speeches, he was always active in the Party's councils.[164] Nevertheless, Twitchell was anything but an unquestioning partisan singing from the Party hymnal. Republican candidates in New Mexico did not always receive his support simply because they were Republicans. When faced with the unscrupulous political machinations of members of his own party, Twitchell was unafraid to speak out and denounce their actions.[165]

This willingness to contravene his own party's political schemes, occasionally set Twitchell at odds with some of New Mexico's Republicans. In the most notable instance, he and party leader Thomas Catron ended up "on less than cordial terms" after an incident in 1892.[166] The problem arose "when Catron appointed Twitchell to a certain local Republican committee," and then "Twitchell did not perform as Catron expected."[167] Furious over the perceived affront, Catron insulted Twitchell, initiating a contentious, recurring feud that colored the pair's personal and political relationship into the twentieth century.[168]

With enemies on both sides of the political divide, Twitchell had to choose his allies extremely carefully. Although he had abandoned his personal political ambitions to elective office after 1892, he never discarded his political agenda. He had a vision for New Mexico: through modernization, along with resource exploitation, and the commodification of the region's diverse cultural past, the territory would become the heart of the United States, capable of dictating "the policies not only of the Southwest, but of the West and with it the Nation."[169] Therefore, he tended to promote individuals with similar goals for the region. Progressive-minded politicians like L. Bradford Prince, and Miguel Otero received tireless support, while those more committed to maintaining the status quo were left wanting.

Statehood was the most salient and enduring of Twitchell's political objectives. For more than two decades, from 1890 to 1912, he worked to procure New Mexico's entry into the Union. In addition to canvassing both the territory and the country to drum up support for the cause, Twitchell backed pro-statehood politicians and promoted the issue from the speaker's platform. He also championed the subject in the press, writing a variety of discourses intended to refute the misconceptions associated with New Mexico and to convince the population of the merits of statehood.

Beginning in 1890, Twitchell and other notable New Mexicans, namely Bernard S. Rodey and L. Bradford Prince, published a number of articles in favor of statehood. A majority of these editorials were written to address concerns about New Mexico's ability to govern itself, a misgiving that had been voiced in opposition to New Mexico statehood as early as 1850.[170] However, not all of the essays Twitchell wrote were directed at those in Washington D.C.; some appealed directly to New Mexicans for support of statehood.

The charge that New Mexicans were incapable of administering to their own governmental needs was nothing more than political posturing, a guileful subterfuge intended to confuse the issue and cloak ulterior motives for blocking New Mexico's bid for statehood. The real reasons behind denying New Mexico statehood had to do with ethnicity and the national balance of power. A large portion of New Mexico's population was either Hispanic and Catholic or Amerindian, all of which were seen by much of the country as foreign and inherently unAmerican. Many eastern politicians doubted the loyalty of these groups and were concerned about the effect that absorbing the region into the Union could have on the power dynamic in Washington D.C. The unfortunate truth of the statehood situation was that New Mexico would have to become more outwardly American and find a way to overcome the sordid details of political partisanship if it was to be successful in its quest for statehood. Ethnic prejudice and discrimination was prevalent throughout American society, stoked by the global imperialist free-for-all taking place toward the end of the nineteenth century. This made statehood a difficult proposition in places like New Mexico that had diverse populations.

Blatant bigotry aside, New Mexico like several other western territories, was being utilized as a pawn in the power struggle between competing political parties. According to Charles Coen, "In congress and in the nation at large, as well as in the territories concerned, the creation of new states has usually been considered from the standpoint, not of national welfare, but of advantage to party, section or locality."[171] Republicans and Democrats were vying for control of the national legislature and the addition of new states, with their accompanying Congressional votes, could mean the difference between the majority and minority position. For this reason neither of the two parties was willing to confer statehood upon a territory unless the newly formed state could strengthen their own influence and power in Congress.

With neither party willing to give way and risk enhancing the efficacy of the opposition, the statehood situation stymied for the balance of the nineteenth century. This shortsighted partisanship frustrated Twitchell, who saw statehood "purely as a business measure" that would benefit all New Mexicans regardless of their political affiliation.172a In his estimation, statehood was imperative and should be brought about by any means necessary, so he publicly advocated bipartisan compromise as a means of getting New Mexico admitted into the Union.172b

A lack of support for statehood among a large portion of New Mexico's population further complicated matters. That, however, was about to change. While serving as a delegate to the Republican National Convention in 1900, New Mexico Governor Miguel A. Otero managed to get an endorsement for statehood incorporated into the party platform. Thereafter, excitement took hold of New Mexico's resident population, and achieving statehood finally appeared to be a real possibility. His resolve buttressed by this modicum of progress, Twitchell redoubled his efforts to promote statehood with his characteristic verve. Despite having recently lost his first wife, Twitchell's desire to see New Mexico become a state remained a priority for him. As the twentieth century began to unfold, Twitchell's enthusiasm for raising the territory's political status began to border on zealotry. In 1901 he made inflammatory statements in an editorial published in the Albuquerque Evening Citizen to the effect that anyone not publicly in favor of statehood should be rooted out and rousted from the territory.[173] Though meant to inspire solidarity and esprit de corps, this outburst turned out to be a miscalculation on Twitchell's part. The comments ended up alienating people and ultimately did very little to further the cause.

Fortunately, Twitchell was not the only New Mexican pulling for statehood. By this time the subject was being discussed and pursued within the territorial government by both Republicans and Democrats, though it would seem never at the same time. In fact, by 1901 the movement for statehood had assumed immense proportions.[174] After Governor Otero and other important individuals succeeded in advancing their statehood agenda at the national level, the campaign gathered a great deal of momentum. For the first time since the Mexican cession, the national political climate appeared to favor statehood for the territories of the Southwest. With both parties apparently favoring the proposition, the outlook for New Mexico statehood had never been brighter.[175] With the goal apparently in sight, New Mexicans fell to sentimentalizing the efforts of those embroiled in the struggle. Jose Francisco Chavez, a former territorial delegate in Congress, was lauded as the father of the statehood movement and honored for his contributions to the cause.[176] Unfortunately, these celebratory claims were premature and statehood still remained just out of reach for New Mexicans as 1901 came to a close.

Statehood might have eluded New Mexico thus far, but its future prospects appeared undiminished. Noted statehood endorser Teddy Roosevelt had become president following the assassination of William McKinley in September 1901, so there was still some level of national backing for the idea, and within the territory support had never been greater. Given these circumstances New Mexico should have been on the fast track to statehood. There were still groups within the territory that opposed becoming a state, however. Many of these coalitions were mercurial and would shift according to changes in the political landscape, which made consensus-building over statehood exceedingly difficult. Years passed with little progress, but Twitchell remained steadfast in his determination. He continued to advocate for statehood and candidates that favored statehood, and his reputation for eloquence preceded him at every political rally.

In 1904, Twitchell supported Republican Bernard S. Rodey's candidacy for New Mexico's delegate to Congress.[177] Like Twitchell, Rodey was an outspoken advocate for New Mexico statehood. He had served as a territorial delegate since the turn of the century, but had been unable to secure the territory's admission into the Union. With dogged determination, he was seeking a third term, intent on gaining statehood by any and all means at his disposal. Rodey even endorsed "jointure," a controversial doctrine that provided for the admission of Arizona and New Mexico as a single state.[178] He supported this idea despite concerns that the massive State would be underrepresented in the Senate. Rodey was convinced that jointure offered the best prospect for achieving statehood, because it assuaged some of the concerns of eastern congressmen worried about the national balance of power shifting to the western states. He was apparently willing to accept disproportionate representation for the inhabitants of the Southwest, if it meant they finally got voting representation in congress. For his part, Twitchell shared this sentiment; he too wanted to secure statehood as quickly as possible and was willing to compromise in order to make it happen. Believing that Rodey was the individual most likely to bring about statehood, Twitchell joined his campaign. The endorsement of a renowned Republican figure like Ralph Twitchell, however, was not enough to win Rodey the nomination. Rodey was defeated in that year's Republican primary by William H. Andrews, an outspoken opponent of jointure.[179]

Unfazed by the downfall of Bernard Rodey, Twitchell continued to advocate for statehood. He sought to align himself with the new territorial delegate William Andrews, a statehood proponent in his own right. Shifting allegiance was not difficult for Twitchell since his focus was on achieving statehood, rather than on any particular candidate or office. In short, he was willing to support anyone who was committed to "helping along the cause of New Mexico's growth."[180]

By 1908, Twitchell was actively campaigning for Andrews, in his bid for reelection as delegate. At a rally for "Statehood and Andrews" in October of that year, Twitchell articulated why he so ardently advocated statehood.[181a] After being introduced by Governor George Curry as "the silver tongued orator of New Mexico: a man well known everywhere but especially in Santa Fe," Twitchell frankly stated, "If there was ever a time, if there ever was a psychological moment in the history of New Mexico, it is now, when statehood is knocking at the gate. To every citizen, no matter what his nativity, or what his politics, has come the momentous question for decision whether or not, he desires the full compliment of American citizenship," Twitchell then reminded the crowd, which consisted of both Democrats and Republicans, that they were not facing a partisan issue, they were deciding "whether or not one star [was] to be added to the American banner."[181b] Before closing with a joke, Twitchell waxed poetic for a spell. Expounding on New Mexico's effulgent destiny he exclaimed, "We are bound to erect an empire that will dictate the policies not only of the Southwest, but of the West and with it of the nation."[181c] He declared this the birthright of every New Mexican, be their name "Gallegos, or Juan Pablo or be it Smith."[181d] His appeal made, Twitchell returned to his seat at the rear of the speaker's platform to listen to his cohorts, and ruminate over the possibility of finally achieving his goal. Unfortunately, despite Andrews' success in the election that followed, New Mexico was left to languish in subordinate status for four more years.[181]e

Finally, on January 6, 1912, President William Howard Taft signed a proclamation making New Mexico the forty-seventh state in the Union. Present at the ceremony was a large delegation of New Mexicans, which may have included R. E. Twitchell. Though he was not an official delegate, he had been one of the main proponents of statehood for over twenty years, and it's reasonable to assume he made the trip to Washington DC for the admission rite.

Following the achievement of statehood, New Mexicans set about the task of deciding upon heraldic emblems for the new state. A competition was held to decide the design of the official state seal and flag. Enticed by the prospect of creating the official symbols of New Mexico, Twitchell submitted a flag for consideration. In creating the design he consulted with a number of individuals and organizations, like the Spanish War Veterans.[182] The standard he designed was a field of light blue, purportedly symbolizing New Mexico's azure skies. The words "New Mexico" printed in white, stretched across the middle of the banner. Boldly emblazoned in the top right corner was the number forty-seven, also in white, denoting New Mexico's entry into the American Union as the forty-seventh state. Opposite these numerals, in the upper left hand corner was Old Glory, the U.S. flag, in full color. The seal of the state, also brightly colored, was stitched in the bottom right corner, above the words "The Sunshine State." A gold fringe hung down the length of the fly.[183] "The Twitchell flag," as it came to be known, was chosen as the first state flag of New Mexico and adopted by the legislature in March 1915.[184]a This flag flew over New Mexico for a decade until it was replaced with the contemporary red and gold zia design in 1925.[184]b

With statehood achieved a major portion of Twitchell's political agenda was fulfilled. Thereafter, his focus shifted to promoting New Mexico and modernizing Santa Fe. Twitchell also remained a centerpiece of the Republican canvassing effort. He continued to promote the party platform, speak in support of like-minded candidates, and organize Republican clubs.

Despite having been out of elective office for almost twenty years, support for R. E. Twitchell to stand as a candidate for any public office was still strong in New Mexico. In 1914, a collection of his friends even tried to compel him to become a candidate for the Republican nomination for Congress. Borrowing from the plot that had successfully landed Twitchell in the Santa Fe mayor's office two decades earlier, the group tried to force Twitchell into running by generating such a groundswell of support for his candidacy that he would be unwilling to refuse. To that end, they published announcements in the regional newspapers claiming Twitchell was receptive to the idea of a congressional run. Twitchell forestalled the campaign before it gathered any real momentum, however, by publishing his own editorial refuting the claim. Regardless of the circumstances, he was determined to carry on his personal boycott against holding elected office.[185]

Content campaigning for others, raising awareness of regional issues, and promoting the Republican Party, Twitchell continued touring New Mexico, speaking to crowds and organizing political clubs through 1916. Thereafter, his priorities shifted from his state to the nation, as the country began to sink into the bloody conflict that was raging around the globe. From 1917 to 1918, the United States was engaged in the First World War, and R. E. Twitchell, then in his late fifties, poured all of his still inexhaustible energies into the war effort. He served foremost as a recruiting officer for the United States Army; his efforts in this capacity were so indefatigable that they were commended in the pages of El Palacio, a periodical in circulation in New Mexico at the time. In support of the war effort he also headed the Committee for the United War Work Campaign, attended the conference of the National War Work Council at San Antonio, and was in charge of the Y.M.C.A. drive for war funds in the Santa Fe district.[186] Additionally, he served on "the Board of Historical Services for the Council of Defense, [and] was largely responsible for the collection and preservation of the state war records."187a Yet, even with all of those responsibilities, Twitchell also found time to serve as Chairman of the Speaker's Bureau. As such, he liberally "employed his famous oratory to enlist volunteers, and arouse enthusiasm for Liberty Loans and meatless meals."187b

The shift to wartime rhetoric undoubtedly came easily for Twitchell. Not only was he a devoted patriot, he also had previous experience with nationalistic rhetoric, albeit twenty years earlier during the Spanish-American War. Back in 1898, he had delivered fiery speeches honoring the country and praising the loyalty and sacrifice of New Mexicans. Naturally, these declamations were highlighted by the exploits and achievements of the U.S. Army First Volunteer Cavalry Regiment, more commonly known as "Roosevelt's Rough Riders."

One of the most famous regiments in American military history, "The Rough Riders" were a collection of young men from around the country who assembled to fight the Spanish in 1898. Imperialistic competition between Spain and the United States had led to war, and a call for volunteers had gone out across America. Men from all walks of life, hungry for glory, rushed to answer President McKinley's appeal for soldiers. Among the respondents were some of the finest horsemen and sharpshooters in the West. Nearly half of those enlisted came from New Mexico. The conflict proved bloody but brief, with the United States defeating the flagging juggernaut in just four months. One of the commanding officers of the American forces, Theodore Roosevelt emerged from the fray a national hero, and his troops became legend, known to history as the "Rough Riders."

New Mexico's Governor Otero had been among those tasked with selecting suitable candidates to fill out the ranks of the Army's First Volunteer Cavalry regiment. Having been appointed Colonel and Judge Advocate General of the Territorial Militia the year before, Ralph Twitchell was the legal advisor to the militia's commander, the governor. As a member of the governor's staff, he assisted in mustering in the contingent of New Mexicans who became famous as Rough Riders.[188] Though the extent of his responsibilities is not entirely clear, when New Mexico's soldiers were assembled in Santa Fe, Twitchell was chosen to receive them on behalf of the governor.[189]

However superficial, this connection placed Twitchell once again in the middle of a historically significant situation. As with his previous military experience chasing fugitive Apaches, circumstances had conspired to place him in contact with a momentous occurrence in United States history. This time, however, Twitchell actually got to meet the famous individual at the center of the incident, the regiment's commanding officer and future President of the United States, Theodore Roosevelt. Whatever his official capacity, Twitchell's involvement with the Rough Riders led to the development of a friendship between the two men. In subsequent years, they corresponded regularly and sought out one another's company whenever they were in the same locale. Roosevelt and Twitchell also became political allies. Twitchell admired Roosevelt a great deal, believing he represented "all that is good and noble in politics."[190] Their relationship, based on mutual esteem, endured until Roosevelt's death in 1919. Even death could not completely sever the ties between these friends, however. After Roosevelt's passing, Twitchell served as his State's chairman for the Roosevelt Memorial Association to honor the tremendous influence his friend had had on the nation that they both labored to develop.[191]

Photographer: Voorhees. Ralph Emerson Twitchell, New Mexico, circa 1898 – 1902.
Courtesy of the Palace of the Governors Photo Archives (NMHM/DCA), #050502

After WWI, Twitchell appears to have gone right back to aiding New Mexico's Republican politicians. He also continued to serve on several of the party's committees as well. In 1920, he was the chairman of the committee charged with arranging the inauguration of the new Republican Governor, Merritt Mechem.[192] That same year, he also served as the "finance chairman of New Mexico for the Republican National Committee during" Warren G. Harding's run for the presidency.[193] He was also one of the delegates from New Mexico at the Republican National Convention.[194]

Following Harding's election, Twitchell applied for a position in the Department of the Interior, a division of the national government devoted to developing the country's natural resources. He was after an appointment as assistant secretary, which he did not get, but New Mexico Senator Albert B. Fall was named Secretary of the Interior, and he gave Twitchell a post within the Interior Department. In May 1921, he was named Special Attorney for the United States Bureau of Mines.[195]

The appointment was hardly a consolation prize. Twitchell had been hand-picked by Secretary Fall and given a "special" assignment that included writing a "history of the Pueblo Indian and a thorough treatise on the Indian land titles in New Mexico."[196] Fall enlisted Twitchell because the latter had long been a student of the history of New Mexico and the greater Southwest. He was well acquainted with the various Native American groups in the region and had actually compiled a lot of the data needed for the assignment prior to his appointment.[197] Twitchell also had decades of experience dealing with land title disputes as a railroad attorney.

By the 1920s conflicts over pueblo lands, brought on by the encroachment of Anglos and Hispanics, were tying up the American court system. Non-Indian settlers were fervently defending claims to lands that legally belonged to the Pueblos. "The courts were swamped with suits to quiet title."[198] From New Mexico, newly appointed Secretary of the Interior Fall was acquainted with the land issues, and he began looking for a way to defuse the situation shortly after taking office. In May 1921, he brought in New Mexico Senator Holm Bursum (his successor in the Senate) to help him craft a solution.[199] Following historical precedent, the duo hatched a plan that was inimical to the interests of the Native Americans involved. The treatise on Native land titles that Twitchell was commissioned to write appears to have factored into the scheme, providing the information needed to devise a way of legitimizing the squatters' claims.

The history of the pueblos that Twitchell wrote for Fall convinced authorities in Washington that he was the expert in the field. This led to an additional appointment of some significance. In August 1921, a scant three months after he was made the Special Attorney for the Bureau of Mines, Twitchell was named United States Assistant Attorney General and put in charge of "looking after the litigation and other legal matters appertaining to the Indians of the Southwest."[200] His duties included reporting "exhaustively and with finality upon the status of land titles within the Pueblo Grants."[201]

Despite the new position, or perhaps because of it, Twitchell's complicity in Fall's land scheme did not end with this study on land rights. Working in conjunction with Commissioner of Indian Affairs Charles Burke, he conducted investigations for Secretary Fall. He also aided Burke and A. B. Renehan, another attorney from New Mexico, in drafting a scandalous measure known as the Bursum Bill. Introduced to the Senate on July 20, 1922 by Senator Bursum, the Bursum Bill, as it came to be called, validated the claims of those Anglo and Hispanic settlers who had held title to pueblo lands for at least a decade prior to 1912. It also included measures that could be used to appropriate the pueblos' water rights.[202]

Twitchell's part in constructing the Bursum Bill varies from account to account. One newspaper lists him as a member of a trio of authors.[203] Another names him as the sole composer of the document.[204] A third source describes him as being "instrumental in drafting the bill at the instance [sic] of Secretary of the Interior Fall."[205] There is no question that he wrote at least a few paragraphs of the document; he admitted as much.[206] He does not appear to have been the principal author, however. In August 1922, Twitchell told The Santa Fe New Mexican that Charles Catron, son of the famous Republican powerbroker Thomas Catron, had written "a great deal of the bill," while he had "prepared the bill and put it in shape to meet the approval of the Indian authorities."[207] Whatever the extent of Twitchell's involvement, it was not his last dealings with the bill.

Thanks to some underhanded manipulation by Bursum, the Senate passed the measure without debate. Word of the bill spread quickly, however, and opposition was forthcoming. With the assistance and support of the General Federation of Women's Clubs, the pueblos hired representation and established a lobby in the capital. They also drafted an appeal that a contingent of tribal leaders conveyed to Washington. Their outcry prompted the Senate to recall the bill from the House of Representatives.[208]

In January 1923, the Senate Committee on Public Lands examined the Bursum Bill in a series of hearings before a subcommittee chaired by Senator Irvine Lenroot.[209] Twitchell's part in the proceedings is somewhat esoteric. Though he appeared in defense of the bill, his testimony ultimately brought about its demise.[210] His involvement in drafting the measure did not preclude him from being able to recognize its shortcomings. He understood how detrimental the proposed legislation was to the pueblos, and explained as much to the Senate sub-committee. When questioned by Senator Lenroot he testified "to the effect that the Bursum bill was not an equitable one for the Indians," and that "it contained radical defects needing correction."[211] He also said that it rendered the pueblos practically helpless, and advocated striking from the document "nearly every passage that would unfairly deprive the Indians of their land."[212] Furthermore, Twitchell stated: "The Indians have been so systematically and persistently robbed by encroachments, false pretenses, and other means by which they have been overreached that somebody has got to be actively representing them."[213] His statements effectively killed the bill.

The defeat of the Bursum Bill was a significant victory for the pueblos, but the title situation remained unresolved. There were still questions surrounding non-Indian claims to pueblo lands. A solution was not far off, however; Congress addressed the issue the following year, passing the Pueblo Lands Board Act in 1924.[214]

Ultimately, the Indian Office claimed responsibility for the drafting and preparation of the Bursum Bill. Still, Twitchell's involvement in the fiasco had some questioning whether he was poorly suited to his job as the appointed legal custodian of Native American interests. Francis Wilson, the attorney who represented the pueblos in their fight against the bill, was quoted in at least one newspaper as saying that he did not believe Twitchell was "the proper person to be representing the Indians."[215] Not everyone was as extreme in their assessment, however. M. K. Sniffen, the secretary of the Indian Rights Association, credited Twitchell for his willingness to amend the bill "where it was found not to be just."[216] Sniffen also acknowledged that Twitchell had "expected hearings would have been held on the measure before it was passed by the Senate."[217] Those in the government believed Twitchell performed the duties of the office well enough. He was continued in the position of special assistant attorney general for several years thereafter, until illness compelled him to resign in 1925.[218]

Twitchell's role in the Bursum Bill scandal was complex. His involvement in preparing the bill affiliated him with the unscrupulous land grabbers that had orchestrated the iniquitous piece of legislation, while his testimony aided in the bill's defeat. There is a chance he endorsed the proposal wholeheartedly at the outset and then changed his thinking with regards to the bill after opposition started to mount. However, there is also no reason to believe he was not simply executing the duties of his office every step of the way. When he was called upon to put the document in order he did so, and likewise when he was called to testify he identified the bill's inequitable shortcomings, fulfilling his responsibility in both instances.

Ultimately, entanglement in the Bursum Bill fiasco tarnished Ralph Twitchell's reputation. His association with the proceedings branded him an adversary of New Mexico's native peoples, which is an unfair assessment considering he was supposed to be defending the measure and instead testified to its inequity. Furthermore, there is absolutely no evidence he stood to gain anything by the passage of the bill. He actually appears to have been little more than a functionary in Secretary Fall's gambit. Yet, his name continues to be attached to the distasteful affair.

Although today he is largely forgotten, in the early twentieth century Ralph Twitchell's "silver tongue" made him one of the most recognizable public speakers in New Mexico. His ability to ensorcel a crowd afforded him the opportunity to remain embedded in New Mexico politics for over thirty years, and his persuasiveness as a speaker made him a highly sought after orator. When called upon Twitchell could be counted on to deliver a message clearly and with conviction. Many New Mexicans relied on him to be their mouthpiece at one time or another.

7

Chief Instigator of Greater Santa Fe

"For the few years that I may still have on earth, I have decided to consecrate myself to furthering the cause of making the capital of New Mexico beautiful."
—Ralph Emerson Twitchell[219]

The ancient capital of New Mexico, Santa Fe, was both Ralph Twitchell's home, and one of the central preoccupations of his life. Though he lived and worked in Las Vegas for many years, Santa Fe was the place he loved and most generously favored with patronage. Captivated by the timeworn city's idyllic surroundings, distinctive architecture, venerable history, and manifold cultural composition, Twitchell devoted himself to making Santa Fe the most magnificent state capital in the country. Regardless of the demands of his legal career or the responsibilities he had to the Republican Party, he was never too busy to assist in efforts to grow and modernize the city, as long as the planned action would not drastically alter the character or appearance of the adobe metropolis. Indeed, Twitchell was extremely concerned about "the preservation of the old customs and old churches and places of interest" around Santa Fe.[220] His affection for the city, in conjunction with his overarching desire to see New Mexico recognized and appreciated as an American wonderland, roused him to give his time and money liberally in support of both urbanization and cultural preservation.

R. E. Twitchell first came to Santa Fe shortly after his arrival in the Southwest to handle some business for the A. T. & S. F. railroad.[221] Quickly becoming enthralled with the place, he immersed himself in the civic matters and communal proceedings of the municipality. As early as March 1884, barely a year after his arrival in the territory, Twitchell was involved in fundraising for local institutions.[222] Over the years that followed the welfare of the city became one of his cardinal concerns. In 1891 he joined the Santa Fe Athletic Club, an organization that aimed to provide the same services to Santa Fe that the Commercial Club did for Albuquerque or Las Vegas.[223] Aggrandizing the city took on such great importance to him that even after swearing off all political offices he was still willing to serve a term as mayor in order to promote the civic modernization efforts that were underway in the early 1890s.

When Twitchell's term as mayor ended in April 1894, Santa Fe was still in the process of urbanizing, paving streets, and constructing modern facilities. As the outbound executive, Twitchell was privy to the city's needs and informed about the pending civic projects. For instance, he was acutely aware that a considerable amount of work still had to be done in constructing the city sewer system. Seizing the opportunity, Twitchell in partnership with his friend Miguel Otero, a prominent Republican who would soon be elected governor, submitted a proposal to the city, soliciting the contract to build the sewers.[224] Twitchell was a shrewd businessman who undoubtedly recognized a chance to profit from the city's development, but he was also a concerned citizen looking to expedite the process of modernization. Santa Fe could not become the gleaming "city on a hill" he envisioned, if a utility infrastructure was not in place. The city council denied his petition, however, electing instead to pass a resolution directing the city engineer to compile a report on the estimated costs of constructing a sewage system.[225]

Denied a sewerage franchise, Twitchell turned his attention to other matters confronting Santa Fe. That same year (1894), the U.S. government closed Fort Marcy, the military post in the heart of the city. This fort was the first American military installation built in the region after the Mexican War. For that reason, the Historical Society of New Mexico deemed it worthy of preservation and moved to have a section of the fort's expansive grounds enshrined as a park and historical site. A stickler for maintaining the historic integrity of Santa Fe and a member of the Historical Society, Twitchell worked to retain part of the fort's acreage as open space. To that end, he created a pamphlet that laid out the history of the fortification (Society Bulletin No. 24). Despite their efforts, the Historical Society was unable to secure any portion of the land "for park and historical purposes."[226] Fort Marcy was left intact under the custody of the Interior Department for nearly a decade before President Theodore Roosevelt turned the fort's roughly seventeen acres over to the Santa Fe Public Schools in 1903.[227]

Through the Historical Society, Ralph Twitchell was frequently involved in community activism because the society regularly "performed labors ... that benefited Santa Fe."[228] One such labor-intensive project was the society's program to acquire what remained of the region's historical artifacts before they disappeared in the steamer trunks of the curio hunters and antiquarians who had been flocking to the area since the arrival of the railroads. "Accumulating varied historical and anthropological materials, [the society] pushed the city to the forefront of the territory in such matters."[229] Twitchell believed so ardently in this work that he actually spent his own money to acquire artifacts and objects d'art for the organization.[230] He presented the society with a number of priceless historical documents, including "a manuscript of De Vargas and a notebook of Manuel Alaverez [sic], who was elected lieutenant governor of New Mexico in 1849."[231] Additionally, he obtained countless antiques, which he also donated, along with several portraits of prominent historical figures relevant to New Mexico that he commissioned from local artists.[232] With the generous contributions of men like Twitchell, the society was able to keep many historical treasures in New Mexico. Indeed, their efforts were so successful that by 1906 the society's collection of relics outstripped the available display space in their offices in the Palace of the Governors.[233]

After years of munificence, members of the Historical Society voted Ralph Twitchell into a position of prominence within the organization. On January 29, 1909, Twitchell was elected vice-president; he was also installed in the office of director. Though the first title was principally an honorary title the later position placed him, for all intents and purposes, in control of the Historical Society. As director he was largely responsible for overseeing the organizational work, securing and preparing historical monographs, collecting and publishing manuscripts, and securing funds within the organization.[234] He continued in that capacity until November 14, 1924, when he was elected president. During his time in charge, Twitchell strove to make the Historical Society the preeminent repository of information concerning New Mexico and the Southwest.[235] His efforts ultimately helped Santa Fe retain its status as the cultural center of New Mexico.

Beyond the Historical Society, Twitchell belonged to several other benevolent organizations and social clubs that tried to preserve the historical integrity of Santa Fe.[236] At the same time, however, he was an active member of the Santa Fe Chamber of Commerce, which was generally involved in promoting the urbanization and commercialization of the city. While this may seem counterintuitive, the two endeavors were actually reconcilable as the binary construct at the heart of Twitchell's vision for the future of Santa Fe, historical tourism.

Santa Fe had been economically depressed since freighting along the commercial highway that shared its name ceased in the late nineteenth century. By the time New Mexico became the forty-seventh state in 1912, the city was in desperate need of a new economic scheme. Having personally been enraptured by the history of New Mexico's capital, Twitchell was convinced that the city's exotic past was interesting enough to attract an un-ebbing flow of sightseers and tourists. Ideally, this steady influx of visitors would provide a new source of income for the city, rejuvenating its economy.

Twitchell was not alone in recognizing that the region's rich history provided fertile material from which to grow a new economy. There was a collective of like-minded residents who were also in favor of capitalizing on their city's historical significance as a way to develop a thriving tourist industry. Many of them were Twitchell's friends and associates from the Archeological Society and the Chamber of Commerce. A few also happened to rank among the state's most influential citizens, including one time governor Miguel Otero and several members of the Santa Fe City Planning Board. This group, organized as the New-Old Santa Fe Committee, Twitchell included, devised a plan for the development of Santa Fe that stressed the importance of preserving the city's oldest structures and thoroughfares. It also recommended that construction within the city be limited to buildings with exteriors that conformed to the "Santa Fe style." Called the "city plan of 1912," the idea was presented to the Santa Fe city council in December of that year.[237]

An outgrowth of the City-Beautiful movement that had been sweeping the nation since the early 1890s, the plan of 1912 aimed to lure in outsiders by making Santa Fe into an attraction.[238] The call to homogenize the city's architecture was an attempt to give the ancient adobe polis a historically immersive quality unlike anywhere else in the country.[239] The New-Old Santa Fe Committee meant to remodel Santa Fe into a romanticized facsimile of its ancient incarnation, a simulacra cityscape with the appearance of historical authenticity. City officials elected not to adopt the plan, but that ended up being inconsequential because public sentiment was squarely behind the idea.[240] Despite the city council's decision, Santa Fe's Chamber of Commerce continued to promote the "Santa Fe style" architecture that was articulated in the plan.[241] In the years that followed, "architectural image became central to stimulating tourism and reversing economic decline" in the city.[242]

Leaving the City-Beautiful model to those communities with a less distinctive idiom, Santa Fe carved out a niche all its own as "The City Different."[243] Boosters took to promoting the city as a place unlike any other. Twitchell, who was the most enthusiastic supporter of the idea, led the charge.[244] He was such an effective booster that The Santa Fe New Mexican once described him as having "done more to give Santa Fe desirable publicity than any other one man."[245]

Ralph Twitchell's commitment to cultivating economic prosperity in Santa Fe was akin to that of a votary. There were no lengths to which he would not go in the name of boosterism. He was even willing to risk life and limb for the mere chance to discuss plans for the city, as he did on June 16, 1914. That evening heavy rains drenched Santa Fe, transforming the streets into torrents more than a foot deep. Floodwaters reached depths approaching four feet in parts of the city. Activity in New Mexico's temporarily subaquatic capital was reduced to only the bravest of impromptu mariners. Common sense dictated that the meeting of the Chamber of Commerce scheduled for eight o'clock that night be cancelled, or at the very least rescheduled, as nobody could be expected to venture out in such a deluge. A number of the chamber's more passionate members were undeterred by the violent downpour, however. Their commitment to boosterism far exceeded their fear of the rising water. All told, twelve plucky enthusiasts, including Twitchell, a faithful janitor, and a couple dutiful reporters, "waded, splashed, stumbled and swam to the Chamber of Commerce meeting," through "the stormy waste of waters."[246]

Under the aegis of dedicated supporters such as these dozen devotees, the Santa Fe Chamber of Commerce provided outstanding advertising for the city.[247] Ralph Twitchell was an integral part of these publicity efforts. He worked diligently to promote the virtues of New Mexico's ancient capital for more than three decades. "Not only during his residence [there] but during some twenty years absence from the city Col. Twitchell had never ceased to regard the welfare and progress of Santa Fe as his paramount interest."[248] In 1916, his efforts earned him the title "Chief of all Boostmasters" from fellow chamber member Frank Owen, as well as a nomination for the chamber's presidency. Concerning the latter, Twitchell demurred, claiming, "he had a great deal to attend to."[249] Nevertheless, he received a third of the votes cast. The other nominee, Judge R. H. Hanna won, but this was of little consequence to Twitchell. His interest was in enhancing Santa Fe, not his own resume. Guided by his sense of propriety, a belief that there ought to be "unanimity in choosing a president," Twitchell moved to make the election of Judge Hanna unanimous.[250]

Regardless of the position he held, or didn't hold, within Santa Fe's Chamber of Commerce, Ralph Twitchell was committed to publicizing the city's many enticements. The same year that he conceded the chamber's presidency to Judge Hanna (1916), he championed establishing a summer military encampment in Santa Fe as a way to advertise the city. Twitchell believed the camp would attract cultured people and generate publicity for the municipality. Indeed, he said as much to The Santa Fe New Mexican in a plea to residents to support the project. While his opinion of newspapers was somewhat guarded, Twitchell often employed public entreaties such as this in his quest to remake Santa Fe. Sometimes it proved to be an effective methodology, in other instances, such as this, it fell short.[251]

When one of Twitchell's civic development suggestions failed to gain traction with the public he did not dwell on missed opportunities, he pragmatically moved on to another project. He cared little about the method used to foster prosperity in the city; his concern was simply that the city prospered. Ralph Twitchell's "greatest ambition was to accomplish something big and permanent for Santa Fe," and he was willing to do whatever it took to accomplish that goal, including ask for help.[252] Just five months after his unsuccessful bid for a military installation in Santa Fe, Twitchell was at it again, imploring the city's residents in the pages of The Santa Fe New Mexican to support another civic enhancement program. This appeal was for assistance with what would turn out to be one of Twitchell's most effective and enduring promotional projects, transforming the city's yearly cultural celebration, la Fiesta De Santa Fe, into "one of the big annual events of the West."[253]

In the early 1900s, the Santa Fe Fiesta was just a small annual gathering held in conjunction with a religious observance that commemorated Don Diego de Vargas and his conquistadors wresting control of the city from the pueblo Indians in 1692.[254] Yet, Twitchell recognized a latent potential in the minor, local rite. He believed that with a little augmentation it could be an attraction capable of luring in tourists from around the country. Within the "simple and purely religious" celebration, Twitchell "saw the dramatic and entertainment possibilities of the Fiesta, and undertook a development plan."[255] As the hypothetical event held the potential to enrich the city and its residents, the idea intrigued many Santa

Feans. A groundswell of excitement eventually led to Twitchell being summoned to the floor of the Chamber of Commerce for an extemporaneous discussion on the subject.

On August 1, 1916, at the monthly meeting of the Santa Fe Chamber of Commerce, Ralph Twitchell was called upon to "make a speech concerning the De Vargas Pageant idea."[256] Though he had not prepared any remarks, Twitchell said that he "was willing to discuss any motion which might be put before the house."[257] He then proposed capitalizing on the city's historical celebration and proceeded to sketch out plans for making the annual Fiesta a lucrative business proposition, similar to Mardi Gras. Twitchell suggested incorporating the De Vargas Pageant Company and allocating funds from the stockholders to cover the initial cost of elevating the festivities to national prominence. He stressed the importance of approaching the endeavor systematically and in a businesslike way and made no attempt to soft-pedal the harsh realities of the proposition. "The project is a big one," he unapologetically declared, "and its successful carrying out will require four or five years," as well as "the expenditure of a great amount of intelligent executive effort, and also no inconsiderable amount of money."[258] A cautionary note that profits were certain to be slim for the first few years followed, but Twitchell assured those listening that with publicity the event would eventually draw people in from around the country, which would increase revenue exponentially and make the enterprise profitable. To emphasize the point he called attention to other cities that had successfully orchestrated cost-effective yearly celebrations of their own. Alluding to the fact that all of these cities relied on sentimentality as the foundation of their festivals, Twitchell made the case that Santa Fe was "richly supplied with sentiment, backed up completely by historical facts," and therefore had "a better reason for celebrating than any other city in the United States."[259]

Intent on making the full scope of his intentions clear, Twitchell stated plainly that a simple street parade would fail to generate widespread interest and would lose money every year. He suggested capitalizing the project with twenty-five thousand dollars to cover the cost of the initial exhibition, namely publicity, music, the acquisition of a suitable location to house the exposition, and most importantly to induce the cooperation of the local Native American tribes. The involvement of New Mexico's indigenous inhabitants was imperative, according to Twitchell, because they were without doubt the biggest draw in the region. When Twitchell finished his remarks, those in attendance enthusiastically carried a motion to appoint an organizing committee. As the originator of the idea, Twitchell was among those selected by the chair to sit on the panel. After the committee had been designated, Twitchell addressed the crowd again delivering an appeal intended to solidify the sense of solidarity permeating the room. With the practiced humility of someone adept at consensus building he said, "he desired to ask most earnestly [for] the support and cooperation of all the people of Santa Fe."[260] He then shifted his tone and called on the members of the chamber directly, and on all good citizens, to aid in publicizing the event. Having placed the onus squarely upon Santa Fe's civic leaders and the community at large, Twitchell offered up one last bit of encouragement, exclaiming, "With all the people striving together to make a success of the big venture, failure will be an utter impossibility."[261]

While the members of the Chamber of Commerce present on that August evening met Twitchell's proposal with enthusiastic support, the Fiesta enterprise failed to gather sufficient momentum outside the half-empty assembly hall. All of Twitchell's ambitious plans for the citywide celebration fell by the wayside. The lukewarm response from residents did little to discourage him, however. He was convinced that the Fiesta De Santa Fe could be made into an iconic event capable of attracting large crowds, so he remained committed to the idea.

With his Fiesta enterprise simmering on a back burner, Twitchell turned his attention to other endeavors. He became the "Chief Instigator of Greater Santa Fe," and began working "to put over a new sewer system; and paving system and lighting system" for the city, as well as "a few boulevards and monuments, bridges and parks."[262] His efforts in this regard were unparalleled, prompting The New Mexican to credit him with initiating the "program of paving, sewerage and street lighting" which the city undertook in 1919.[263] That year, the city council passed an initiative calling for the paving of "some thirty blocks, including practically all the heart of the city."[264a] The bill also included provisions for enlarging the municipal sewer system, and grading the "principle streets in the outlying parts of the city."[264b]

When the project hit a snag, R. E. Twitchell was called upon to assist in the huge public works improvement campaign. Twitchell, who was "the chief moving spirit among the property owners for paving improvements," was appointed "special counsel to the mayor [E. P. Davies], alderman and city attorney in the handling of all legal and technical matters connected with the paving program."[265] The council turned to him for help when legal issues requiring immediate attention cropped up while the city attorney was out of town. His entanglement in the project quickly escalated, however, after he agreed to help the finance committee prepare a city budget.[266] Involvement was certainly no hardship for him; making New Mexico's capital city great had been a goal of his for many years and he undoubtedly saw this municipal improvement project as a step in that direction.

Ralph E. Twitchell, Santa Fe, New Mexico, January 1919. Photographer: Wesley Bradfield. Courtesy of the Palace of the Governors Photo Archives (NMHM/DCA), #013432

By 1919, there was finally enough support from Santa Feans to commence with the Fiesta project Twitchell had laid out three years earlier, albeit on a somewhat smaller scale. Presumably, the prospect of an economic boom was just too seductive for the city's residents to ignore any longer. On April 24, 1919 "four committees, from the Women's club, the Women's Board of Trade, the Community theatre, and the Chamber of Commerce, met at the museum to discuss the proposition of putting on a Santa Fe pageant" later that year, "and every year thereafter."[267] Those present at the meeting came to the conclusion that such an event "could and would be produced" before the year's end.[268] They decided that the purpose of the first year's event would be "to make a modest beginning, for it was agreed that the first few productions would not pay expenses."[269] The meeting adjourned after the attendees agreed to encourage their various organizations to "get behind this pageant and assist in its production by every means in their power."[270]

Having made the decision to move forward with the historically themed event, planning and preparations began, but without a blueprint to follow much of it had to be extemporized. "The first Fiesta was more or less impromptu," orchestrated "under the direction of a handful of people," and "put on at a total expense of only a few hundred dollars."[271] Furthermore, "it was not widely advertised."[272] Yet, the event turned out to be "a brilliant, picturesque, clever and beautiful performance" that demonstrated Santa Fe's ability to stage a successful public celebration.[273]

During the last week of June 1919, representatives from "civic associations and institutions" met with the Santa Fe Chamber of Commerce several times to draw up an outline for the prospective Fiesta.[274] The plan that was ultimately adopted outlined a three-day festival with performances and events portraying a thousand years of New Mexico history. Arrangements for a "formal Peace Celebration" acknowledging the end of the world war that had recently reached a conclusion were also included.[275] The position of Fiesta Director went to a gentleman named Roscoe Hill, who immediately set about locating the costumes that had been used in a rendition of the De Vargas pageant back in 1912.[276] Since De Vargas' reconquest of Santa Fe took place in the middle of September, the dates designated for the Fiesta were September eleventh through the thirteenth.[277]

As August rolled into September Santa Fe was abuzz with excitement. Word had gotten around that tourists were expected to come from as far away as the East Coast, "and assurance [had] been given that the dwellers from Roswell to Raton, from Albuquerque to Las Vegas and beyond, [would] motor to Santa Fe for the occasion."[278]

In the days leading up to the 1919 Fiesta de Santa Fe a large stage was constructed in the Plaza by the Santa Fe Carpenter's Union, who had "agreed to build the platform as a gift to the community."[279] A series of "booths built of aspen poles and cedar and pinion boughs" were also erected in the square.[280] Business owners and residents were urged, "to throw their flags to the breezes" and to hang "bunting and other decorations" around town.[281] The city started to fill up with tourists as well, many of who were New Mexicans that had come aboard railcars from around the state.[282]

On the evening of September 10, 1919, a profusion of Native Americans from all over New Mexico began descending on Santa Fe. They were to be featured performers in the Fiesta, the first day of which was devoted to the region's aboriginal heritage. Well into the night, by the half-light of the moon, "wagon after wagon and horseman after horseman drew up in the city."[283] More New Mexico tribesmen arrived the following morning, swelling the already crowded streets "thronged with cowboys, Indians, visitors from nearby plazas and with tourists."[284]

The first day's events consisted of a variety of Native American ceremonies and dances, which included races and dramatic plays. Beyond the exploits of the native tribesmen, the city's "restaurants were crowded and merchants seemed to be doing a thriving business."[285]

Day two was 'Spanish Day' and was "dedicated to the Franciscans and the Conquerors."[286] The festivities resumed around 10:00 a.m. with the erection of a large cross in the plaza, which was accompanied by the chanting of "a Te Deum in Gregorian measure" by the Franciscans, and followed by a reenactment of Don Diego de Vargas' reconquest of the city, with Santa Fe Sheriff George W. Armijo playing the lead role.[287] After the ceremony a tea garden was set up to provide the crowd with refreshments, and later in the afternoon Spanish dances were performed for the patrons of the Plaza Market. Attendees were then treated to a thrilling mock stagecoach robbery, and an exhibition of "typical cowboy sports."[288] The evening's entertainment included staged assassinations and stick-ups, and then concluded with an extravagant ball.[289]

The final day of the Fiesta focused on New Mexico as a part of the United

States, and included a celebration of America's victory in the First World War.[290] A reenactment of General Stephen Watts Kearny's bloodless takeover of Santa Fe was also presented to "a large and appreciative crowd."[291] During the evening rain set in, disrupting the final performances, sending the performers and spectators scurrying for cover. Impromptu arrangements were made "to transfer such part of the evening's entertainment as it was feasible to give in doors to the St. Francis auditorium," where the Fiesta wrapped up with a few more Native American and Spanish dances, and a performance by The Liberty Chorus.[292]

By and large, residents deemed the first "revised" Fiesta de Santa Fe an overwhelming success, and many were ready to get behind the idea of holding the event on an annual basis. About a month after the proceedings, at a banquet held at the museum, the city's businessmen voted unanimously in support of the idea, and agreed "to raise a guarantee of $2,500," for the purpose of underwriting the next year's Fiesta.[293] Twenty of the more enthusiastic financier's present pledged fifty dollars each right there on the spot.[294]

Among those gathered at the museum banquet that October evening was Ralph Twitchell. He was actually seated at the head table and was one of the night's featured speakers. When the topic of the Fiesta was introduced "Twitchell was called upon first, as a master builder and city planner, and he summed up the case for the Fiesta in eloquent and persuasive manner."[295] He also "outlined a feasible financial plan and recommended the incorporation of an organization to be known simply as the 'Santa Fe Fiesta.'"[296] The speakers that followed Twitchell all shared his sentiments, and when the speechmakers were finished the crowd united in support of making the Fiesta an annual occurrence.[297]

Despite the initial thousand-dollar outlay from the city's boosters, the second annual Fiesta De Santa Fe was still desperately under-funded as 1919 gave way to 1920. The project's economic deficiencies were not enough to quell the momentum that had built up behind the idea, however. Another musical exposition had already been added to the program, and topics pertaining to the upcoming event had infiltrated the dockets of civic organizations other than the Chamber of Commerce.[298] The success of the event the previous year had made many Santa Feans more inclined to support the Fiesta. By April, nearly the entire community was behind the endeavor. Attendance at Chamber of Commerce meetings swelled, and the public's enthusiasm grew palpable.

As one of the architects of the enterprise, Ralph Twitchell was at the epicenter of the excitement surrounding the Fiesta. Many Santa Feans had come to associate him with the venture, and to believe that he was the right individual to bring the elaborate exposition to another successful conclusion. Twitchell's virtually unparalleled understanding of the historical significance of the city made him uniquely qualified to take over the project, and even his detractors were in agreement that he was "a man of broad vision," one who had "a grasp of big things."[299]

Overwhelmingly confident in Twitchell's abilities, the townspeople maneuvered to give him control over the Chamber of Commerce, which was largely responsible for staging the event. On the evening of April 6, "at the largest and most enthusiastic meeting of the Santa Fe Chamber of Commerce for years," Santa Feans unanimously elected Twitchell president, effectively empowering him to sculpt the Fiesta in accordance with his vision.[300]

Twitchell gratefully accepted the presidency in a short speech that detailed his larger objectives. After underscoring "that the capital of New Mexico and its possibilities was his chief hobby," he elaborated on his goal of orchestrating a concerted effort among cities in New Mexico, led by Santa Fe, to make the state's capital "one of the most beautiful in the country."[301] He then urged Santa Feans to take the initiative, and enlist the cooperation of the rest of the state by demonstrating the effectiveness of an unassailably solid, cooperative campaign in the days ahead. Before ending his speech, Twitchell praised those present, remarking that he had never before seen so much interest in the city's welfare.[302]

Later in the meeting, Twitchell returned to the lectern to outline plans for the forthcoming Fiesta. First, he suggested the formation of "a board of governance for the Fiesta composed of representatives of all civic organizations, the city and the museum."[303] He then went over a strategy for financing the event. "The plan [was] to make all the Fiesta attractions except the music and street parades paid affairs," with local citizens covering the initial costs by advancing money in fifty and hundred dollar increments that would be "repaid from the sale of concessions and gate receipts."[304] The idea appears to have been well received by the throng. That night, a committee was appointed to secure the needed capital, and the organization of a board of Fiesta managers was outlined. When the meeting adjourned the Santa Fe Fiesta was well on its way to becoming the marquee event Twitchell had conceptualized.[305]

On June 26, 1920 the Fiesta was formally placed under the control of the board of directors of the Chamber of Commerce.[306] A month later the Chamber was devoting twelve hours a day to the enterprise, and its efforts were yielding results. Everyone in Santa Fe seemed "to be getting the Fiesta fever."[307]

With six weeks left to prepare, Twitchell, who had been named Fiesta Director, had his organization running smoothly down to the smallest detail. Promotional literature was placed in all of the railway stations in the state, and the A. T. & S. F. Railroad agreed to devote the entirety of the August 1920 issue of their monthly bulletin to an elaborate, illustrated Fiesta advertisement. The replica armor and weapons needed to outfit several companies of faux conquistadors for the reenactment was under construction, as was the grandstand, and tickets were available for purchase. The preparations were departmentalized, but no aspect of the project fell beyond Twitchell's purview, because all expenditures required his written approval.[308]

Ralph Twitchell's desire to make the 1920 Fiesta an unqualified success compelled him to go way beyond simply fulfilling his obligations as director. The seasoned genealogist tracked down as many of "the descendents of the Conquerors" as he could, and arranged for them to take part in "the big Pageant Parade."[309] He also visited Tesuque, Cochiti, and San Ildefonso, along with assistant director Lansing Bloom, to make "arrangements for the participation of the Indians."[310] To accommodate the tremendous glut of tourists expected to flood the city, he contacted the state highway department and arranged for the use of some tents.[311] What's more, authenticity was extremely important to him, so when he was unable to acquire everything he needed for the event within New Mexico, Twitchell traveled to Chicago to secure costumes, and to El Paso to obtain sombreros.[312]

The costumes Twitchell was collecting were not only for use in the De Vargas pageant/reenactment, but also for a play he had written based on "the trial by court martial before" De Vargas, "of the Indian governors of the pueblos of Namba and Santo Domingo and two pueblo warriors on the charge of treason."[313] Taking "parts from the musty archives of the Spanish occupation without the changing of a word," Twitchell created a production that "brought into prominence the most intensely dramatic points of the trial."[314] He "wouldn't permit any anachronism to creep into the affair-not even in the costuming-and he spent some time rounding up costumes of the style of the later part of the seventeenth century for his actors."[315]

The project proved to be no small affair, but by the time it was finished Twitchell was certain no one could "pick a flaw anywhere in the drama from the standpoint of faithful reproduction of the manners and customs of the time of De Vargas."[316] Historical accuracy was of the utmost importance to him, and he conveyed as much to his actors. He wanted to reenact the events of the past as closely as possible and expected them to know their lines perfectly. One performer mused that unlike the previous year, every actor had to "be letter perfect," and every performance had to "be rehearsed thoroughly from beginning to end."[317]

Twitchell was doing everything he could think of "to make this Fiesta the biggest thing ever connected with Santa Fe."[318] He even arranged an advertising campaign that broadcast the event across the state via one of the technological marvels of the time, the airplane. In the month preceding the Fiesta, the Cassell Motor Company was contracted "to make flights over the different cities of the state and drop out bombs" loaded with promotional material.[319] Airplanes had never been employed in an advertising capacity in New Mexico prior to this instance.[320]

In the interest of making the 1920 Fiesta de Santa Fe an even more memorable spectacle, Twitchell also sponsored the erection of a monolithic work of art, dubbed the Cross of the Martyrs, which was planted on a hill north of the plaza and designated the terminus of the candle light procession intended to conclude the festivities.[321] A twenty-five foot tall reinforced concrete crucifix that Twitchell actually had a hand in designing, the Cross of the Martyrs was a memorial to the Franciscan Friars who were killed by Native Americans during the Pueblo Revolt in 1680. During the Fiesta the seventy-six ton statue was dedicated in a ceremony that drew a mass of onlookers, and the candlelight cortege from the plaza to the cross became an annual ritual.[322]

By September tourists were accumulating on the streets of Santa Fe, and the Chamber of Commerce was fielding questions about the impending Fiesta every day.[323] When the proceedings finally commenced on September thirteenth there were "hundreds of visitors in the city."[324] Like the preceding year's event, the 1920 Fiesta de Santa Fe was a rousing success. As Twitchell had predicted, tourists flocked to the ancient city, lured in by the mystique of the conquistador and the Indian. An estimated three thousand people attended the event.[325] The considerable turnout exceeded expectations, as well as the seating capacity of the grandstand. At many of the performances standing room was sold to individuals who were unable to secure seats. Though it fell short of being profitable, the Fiesta enterprise showed tremendous moneymaking potential, which made it less difficult to find guarantors for the 1921 Fiesta. Indeed, planning began for the next year's exhibition almost immediately.[326]

The success of the 1920 Fiesta assured Ralph Twitchell's re-election as president of the Santa Fe Chamber of Commerce, and his retention as director of the Fiesta. A week after the conclusion of the 1920 affair, he "was unanimously elected director for the 1921 Fiesta."[327] Still bent on making that event the hallmark of the city, Twitchell was more than happy to shoulder the administrative duties for another year. His plan for the celebration had always been a multi-year program designed to expand and grow as the publicity from each successive year's festivities generated more and more interest.

Building on the achievements of the previous year, Twitchell orchestrated another noteworthy Fiesta in 1921, demonstrating that the festival was indeed the city's most promising enterprise. Promotional material distributed by the Chamber of Commerce succeeded in enticing people from all across the country to travel to Santa Fe in September 1921.[328] A final tally indicated visitors from thirty-one different States made the pilgrimage that year.[329] The escalation in attendance brought the enterprise to the brink of solvency. When the year's Fiesta accounts were settled the outstanding debts amounted to less than five hundred dollars.[330]

The small financial shortcoming notwithstanding, most Santa Feans judged the 1921 Fiesta de Santa Fe to be a tremendous success. Acknowledged as the catalyst behind that success, Ralph Twitchell was praised for his skilful management of the elaborate commemorative extravaganza. The Santa Fe New Mexican hailed his imagination and enthusiasm as the reason for the project's continued advancement, and many of the city's residents felt they owed the enterprising administrator a debt of gratitude for his effort, vision, passion, and ingenuity as the "chief spirit" of the event. This sense of indebtedness obliged a group of appreciative citizens to raise over two hundred dollars for the purpose of making a grand gesture showing their gratitude. On October 14, 1921, this assemblage of thankful denizens presented Twitchell with a token of their esteem, an oil painting by Gerald Cassidy, one of his favorite local artists.[331]

Not everyone in Santa Fe was as excited about the Fiesta enterprise as the committee that gifted the painting to Ralph Twitchell, however. A number of residents saw the extravagant remembrance as a costly, overblown gimmick that had been foisted upon them by a Chamber of Commerce they perceived as superfluous. These dissenters held their tongues while the city basked in the afterglow of the festivities, but once the sheen faded they began to convey their discontent. What is more, the complaints were not limited to the Fiesta venture alone; the Santa Fe Chamber of Commerce was the real object of their grievances.

In February 1922, a representative of one of the city's most prominent business institutions informed R. E. Twitchell that the Chamber of Commerce only enjoyed his institution's support because it was "a sort of necessary evil."[332] These sentiments shocked and offended Twitchell, to say the least. He was of the opinion that a Chamber of Commerce served as "the foundation stone of civic prosperity," and could not understand why the city's principal business owners were not the biggest supporters of the organization.[333] The overt hostility toward the civic cooperative he had chaired for the preceding two years was exasperating, if not insulting. After years of working to generate wealth and prosperity in the isolated city, Twitchell was unwilling to tolerate this affront. He immediately drafted a letter to the Chamber's Board of Directors tendering his resignation. The document explained that he would no longer serve as either president of the institution or director of the Fiesta, because he refused to be associated with any "necessary evil."[334a] Twitchell cited Santa Fe residents' indifference "to the importance of having a live chamber of commerce" as his main reason for quitting, and then added, "The [Chamber's] membership, with a few notable exceptions, will not do its share of the public work."[334b]

Twitchell's resignation was cause for concern to the Santa Feans who recognized the merits of the Fiesta celebration and the Chamber of Commerce. Not only was he the driving force behind the resurgent historical observance, he had spent the past two years trying to infuse energy and excitement into the Chamber.[335] He could not be easily replaced. Recognizing how significant losing Twitchell's guidance was for the city, The Santa Fe New Mexican moved quickly to support him, lauding his efforts to make the Fiesta enterprise a success, and saying that "it would be unfortunate were he allowed to relinquish the job" of Fiesta Director.[336] Any anxiety concerning Twitchell's abdication was dispelled after only a few weeks, because he willingly returned to the fold, his indignation superseded by his sense of civic responsibility and the reassurance proffered by some in the community. The Chamber's membership celebrated Twitchell's return by voting him the organization's president for a third consecutive year and reinstalling him as the director of the Fiesta De Santa Fe.[337]

Picking up where he left off, Twitchell resumed his efforts to make the Fiesta a prosperous national attraction. In an attempt to increase attendance he expanded the advertising campaign. Most notably he negotiated a deal with the Fred Harvey Company, famous for their vast array of restaurants, hotels, and railroad dining cars, to distribute a "series of ten Santa Fe Fiesta poster-postcards by Artist Gerald Cassidy."[338]

Laboring in the face of a largely apathetic populace, Ralph Twitchell, aided by a few like-minded administrators, made the 1922 Fiesta De Santa Fe a spectacular extravaganza that surpassed the two previous years fetes in both pageantry and splendor. Many of the kinks that had disrupted the proceedings in prior years had been addressed, and the program was transfigured to include more elements of New Mexico's historical progression. The grandeur of the opening day performances alone prompted The Santa Fe New Mexican to declare the exposition "a marvelous achievement" that had been "established for all time as one of the premier pageantry events of the world."[339]

Once again the celebration fell short of being remunerative, but the gate receipts from the three-day gala showed an increase in attendance that bespoke a future profitability.[340]

After the 1922 exposition there were no longer any doubts about whether the Fiesta and the Chamber of Commerce were worthwhile enterprises. The obvious commercial benefits the duo bestowed upon the city had silenced the critics and sparked a surge in community support. More than a hundred citizens attended a Chamber of Commerce "Fiesta Dinner," held two weeks after the observance, to discuss the achievements of the 1922 event and the prospects for the next year. During that banquet Ralph Twitchell was lionized for his part in making the Fiesta De Santa Fe a singular attraction. The Reverend W. S. Trowbridge hailed him as a "dreamer" who was able to make "his visions materialize," and lauded his "dramatic instinct and store of historical knowledge," as well as "his determination to 'go ahead despite knockers.'"[341] The good reverend then drove his point home with the simplest of statements: Ralph Twitchell is the Chamber of Commerce. Twitchell, secure in the knowledge of his accomplishments, humbly rebutted the clergyman's tribute. He claimed "that the big work for the chamber was done quietly by the directors and praised Edgar L. Street for his faithful and efficient work on that behalf."[342] There was more than enough room in the spotlight for everyone who had helped put on the Fiesta.

For reasons unknown, Ralph Twitchell chose not to officiate over either the Santa Fe Chamber of Commerce or the Fiesta De Santa Fe in 1923. He does not appear to have left under duress, and in all likelihood, he probably could have held on to either or both of the positions were he so inclined. Apparently, he was satisfied that the Fiesta was established on a secure footing and was therefore willing to relinquish control to someone else. After moving aside, Twitchell certainly did not divorce himself from the chamber or the Fiesta, he continued to promote the event and the organization. The publicity booklet issued by the chamber for the 1925 Fiesta prominently featured "a history of the palace of the governors, written by Ralph Emerson Twitchell."[343]

When Ralph Twitchell opted to reduce his role in producing the Fiesta De Santa Fe, he left the enterprise in full swing and just shy of solvency. The annual celebration was attracting tourists and historical enthusiasts from virtually the entire country.[344] It was also beginning to lure an assortment of sightseers, students, and artists from Europe.[345] Many of the logistical details related to putting on the extravagant festival had already been addressed and were no longer a concern. Namely, a large stage and amphitheatre had been constructed so as to be reusable every year.[346] The Fiesta organization had borrowed money to cover its costs, but had paid off most of the debt while Twitchell was still in office, so the enterprise was financially stable as well.[347] Through skillful management Twitchell had built-up the all but forgotten rite into a solidly entrenched institution with tremendous commercial growth potential. His successor just had to keep the ball rolling.

Artfully crafted, extensively publicized, and thoroughly ingrained in the collective consciousness of residents, the Fiesta De Santa Fe continued to grow and flourish after R. E. Twitchell disengaged himself from the proceedings. "As Santa Fe's artists and creative community began playing a greater role in organizing Fiesta in the 1920s, events such as the pet parade (originally an animal show), the 'hysterical' parade, and the burning of Zozobra, artist Will Schuster's giant effigy of gloom, were added to the celebration."[348] A number of the elements Twitchell had incorporated into the proceedings, such as the candlelight procession to the Cross of the Martyrs, are still part of the annual event today. The terminus of the succession has shifted to a less urban location (the original cross still stands on a promontory in what is now a residential neighborhood), and the closing ceremony is now held beneath a somewhat less impressive rood, but the spirit of the ritual is the same. Though the event changed over time, Santa Fe's annual extravaganza is still one of the city's grandest expositions. Ralph Twitchell had indeed achieved something transcendent and enduring for the city he loved.

8
Chief of All Boostmasters

"Hell, there are no rules here—we're trying to accomplish something."
—Thomas Edison

Employment opportunities may have lured Ralph Emerson Twitchell to New Mexico, but it was the region's distinctive landscape and colorful history that captivated his imagination and cultivated his affections for the region. Fascinated by the manifold beauty of his surroundings, Twitchell spent countless hours roaming over the territory's austerely picturesque topography, seeking out the decaying edifices of ancient civilizations or retracing the footsteps of conquistadors. He was even inspired by the scenic majesty to take up both photography and archaeology. His love affair with New Mexico, however, went well beyond sightseeing and leisure activities. Twitchell became one of New Mexico's most enthusiastic patrons, taking an interest in everything from reclamation to the highway system, and seizing every opportunity to espouse the region's latent potential to anyone who would listen. As a spokesman Twitchell was second to none, and his tireless efforts "did much to dramatize the unique character of New Mexico."[349]

Struck by the comeliness of his surroundings, Twitchell envisioned a future for New Mexico that was a dramatic departure from the extractive paradigm of the majority of his predecessors. In his vision, the state's resources would be exploited for the sake of the state, instead of for the enrichment of outside interests. While many of his contemporaries were looking only at what they could extract from the land, he perceived of an inherent connectivity in the land and understood that it was a transferable commodity of sorts. The scenic vistas, storied history, and trichotomous cultural composition of New Mexico and the greater Southwest, made it a wonderland of kaleidoscopic beauty unlike anywhere else in the world, a place to experience rather than just a thing to take apart. Twitchell was convinced that if New Mexico's natural resources were developed and its virtues widely publicized, then the region could lure in people from around the country, which would bolster the local economy. Over time, this belief became his central preoccupation.

While in pursuit of Geronimo and his comrades during the summer of 1885, R. E. Twitchell had been able to see much of New Mexico. Out in the field he had paid close attention to the parched landscape of his new home, and took note of its limited carrying capacity. His observations convinced him that the harshness of the terrain, its petrous soil and scant water supply, restricted the growth of everything from plant life, to population, to industry. Twitchell realized that the development of the Southwest would be predicated in large part on the availability of water, so he became actively concerned with reclamation. By 1889 he was regularly "identified with irrigation and conservation matters."[350]

In 1891, a collection of representatives from the arid western states assembled in Salt Lake City, Utah, to petition the national government for an increase in the amount of control the individual states could exercise over the country's western water supply.[351] It was the initial meeting of the National Irrigation Congress (NIC). The attendees hoped to convince the national legislature that it would be in the country's best interest to allow the inhabitants of America's western lands to harness the region's waterways and redirect them to serve agricultural and commercial purposes. Roughly four hundred and fifty delegates attended the first NIC.[352] The meeting brought greater attention to irrigation issues in the West and thrust conservation efforts into the national spotlight.

Only a small contingent of New Mexicans traveled to Utah for the inaugural NIC, because the New Mexico Territorial Fair was being held at the same time. This left New Mexico woefully underrepresented at the event. To ensure that New Mexicans stayed abreast of any developments in the field of reclamation, and to continue the work initiated by the NIC, Governor L. Bradford Prince called for a Territorial Irrigation Convention to be held in Las Vegas in March of the following year. This conference was essentially an extension of the Salt Lake City proceedings with basically the same goal: to influence national legislation. Given the success of the NIC, expectations for the Territorial Convention at Las Vegas were extremely high. The event did not disappoint; attendance failed to equal what was anticipated, but there was a sizable turnout. Roughly three hundred delegates, representing the territory and neighboring states, took part.[353]

Governor Prince appointed Ralph Twitchell to serve on the Santa Fe County delegation.[354] Though the specifics of his contribution are murky, it appears that he may have had a hand in arranging the whole affair. A stray reference to him organizing "the first irrigation congress" appeared in one of his many obituaries.[355] Furthermore, a biographical sketch of R. E. Twitchell, written in 1916, credits him with having been the originator of many "general movements for the development and progress of the West."[356]

There was no NIC convention held in 1892, but the organization reconvened a year later and continued to meet annually thereafter for more than two decades, except in 1901. Though Ralph Twitchell may have been involved with the group as early as the mid-1890s, there is no substantial evidentiary connection between him and the NIC prior to the twentieth century. His first confirmed involvement with the congress was as a member of the New Mexico delegation that attended the eleventh session of the NIC, held at Ogden, Utah, in 1903.[357]

In 1904 and 1905 the NIC met in El Paso, Texas, and Portland, Oregon, respectively. Twitchell was probably present at both events, but his name escaped mention in the newspaper coverage. In any case, his previous experience and knowledge of the subject matter put him on the short list of individuals the governor would have considered for appointment when the New Mexico delegations were being assembled.

If Twitchell was left off the delegation in either 1904 or 1905, his absence was brief. His name reappears in connection with the NIC in 1906. That year he represented New Mexico during the fourteenth session of the congress in Boise, Idaho.[358] He was something more than just a delegate this time, however. He had the added task of petitioning the congress to hold its next session in New Mexico. That year, three states and a territory lined up their "cleverest orators to urge their claims" to the forthcoming session, and Twitchell was selected to argue for making Las Vegas the next host city.[359] Given his widely acknowledged oratorical prowess, he undoubtedly made a strong case for holding the event in the meadow city, but in the end, he was unable to secure the congress for New Mexico. The honor of hosting the fifteenth session of the NIC ultimately went to Sacramento, California.

Losing out on the congress was a disappointment, but New Mexico's irrigation and reclamation interests had plenty to celebrate. 1906 had already been an auspicious year for irrigation/reclamation in the territory; an agreement had been reached with Mexico concerning water use that allowed for an overhaul of the region's main river system.[360] The settlement set plans into motion to construct a dam on the Rio Grande that would greatly expand the agricultural productivity of New Mexico's heartland. Twitchell was at the center of the proceedings. He "was chairman of the Rio Grande Commission, which drew up the treaty between the United States and Mexico and resulted in the building of the Elephant Butte Dam in New Mexico."[361]

Ralph Twitchell attended the 1907 NIC in Sacramento as a member of the New Mexico delegation and as a representative of the A. T. & S. F. Railroad.[362] That August, he set out for California, "Armed with thousands of circulars and loaded down with photographs," intending to promote "Las Vegas and the adjacent farming country with all his might."[363] The pictures were of the city and surrounding area, and were meant to show off the resources of New Mexico's northern tablelands. They included scenes of grain and other agricultural products growing and being harvested, as well as images of wild uncultivated lands and coursing mountain streams. The Las Vegas Daily Optic called them "probably the finest set of photographs in the country."[364]

Though information about the 1907 event is limited, there are indications that Twitchell factored in prominently. On the last day of the conference, when provisions were being made for the next session, Twitchell was elected Secretary of the Board of Control for the succeeding year's convocation.[365] After the managing committee had been selected, a host city was designated. As in the previous year, Twitchell was the individual responsible for arguing New Mexico's case to host the next NIC. He was not advocating for Las Vegas again; this time he spoke on behalf of Albuquerque. The reason New Mexico chose to assert Albuquerque rather than Las Vegas is unclear. Perhaps, the previous year's experience had convinced those involved that NIC officials did not find Las Vegas an attractive enough site. Regardless of these particulars, Twitchell had once again been charged with securing the NIC for New Mexico. Drawing on all his oratorical skill and flair, he delivered a speech that ranked among the finest he had ever given. A member of the California delegation present at the conference said that Twitchell's speech "was the best, most impressive and most convincing he had ever heard and that it changed him completely from being in favor of another place to vote for Albuquerque."[366] When he was finished the assemblage chose Albuquerque as the site of the sixteenth NIC.

As secretary, Twitchell was in charge of arranging the proceedings of the NIC in 1908.[367] Playing host to the NIC was an opportunity for New Mexico to showcase its bounty to the world. Cognizant of that fact, R. E. Twitchell tried "to do something for the material welfare of the entire territory."[368] He envisioned putting on the grandest session in the history of the congress to increase New Mexico's national valuation. First and foremost, his plan required funds. To raise money he traveled to Washington D. C. at his own expense, to work with NIC Chairman W. S. Hopewell, Territorial Governor George Curry, and Congressional Delegate William Andrews in securing a $30,000 appropriation from the federal government to cover "the maintenance and expense" of hosting the expo.[369] While in the nation's capital the foursome also managed to procure an additional outlay of $30,000 to supplement the construction of a new federal building in Albuquerque.[370]

With funding taken care of, Twitchell was free to focus his attention on promoting the event. To draw as many visitors as possible, he broadcast news of the conference all over the West. "He was a born advertiser and showman," as well as a lover of "the spectacular and the light of publicity."[371] Taking a comprehensive approach, he arranged to have news of the sixteenth National Irrigation Congress and Interstate Industrial Exposition published in roughly three thousand newspapers around the country.[372] He prepared alluring brochures that promoted the unique character of the state.[373] He also "compiled his first big volume on the resources of New Mexico."[374] His plan included advertising through the Denver and Rio Grande railroad's passenger department as well, which he saw to, personally.[375] Additionally, he and Chairman Hopewell, aided by an army of clerks, sent out "all sorts of promotional literature to the various executive committeemen and others prominently identified with irrigation matters in the seventeen states and territories under the Reclamation Act," which was a Federal law enacted to encourage the "reclamation" of arid western lands for agricultural purposes.[376] He even went so far as to inform several foreign governments of the affair.[377]

Twitchell also traveled around New Mexico and the adjacent states stirring up interest and gathering support. Enlisting help from the southern reaches of New Mexico he obtained $300 from the Las Cruces Chamber of Commerce to pay for promotional literature.[378] In Arizona he met with Governor Joseph Kibbey to discuss that state's interest in the event. He also arranged to have a mineral exhibit transported from Phoenix to Albuquerque.[379] On a trip to Colorado he enlisted the support of the delegates of a cattlemen's convention and spent several days speaking to those in attendance trying to lure them to Albuquerque.[380]

To make attending the festivities affordable for everyone in New Mexico, Twitchell negotiated a decrease in railway rates with the Santa Fe railroad. His influence with the rail company officials was vitally important in securing this concession. No body else in the congress could have accomplished such a feat.[381] The rail companies were notoriously difficult to elicit help from, but Twitchell knew exactly "how to pull the tough legs" of the officials.[382]

Extensive preparatory measures were undertaken to ready Albuquerque for the twelve-day extravaganza. A new convention hall was raised, the University of New Mexico's classrooms were filled with irrigation exhibits, and the streets downtown were bedecked with thousands of colored lights.[383] A massive tent city, capable of accommodating more than 5,000 people was erected, and the city's rail yards were cleared to make room for hundreds of Pullman cars.[384] Not wanting to miss a moment of the proceedings, Governor Curry temporarily relocated his home and office to the city.[385]

People from all over the world converged on New Mexico for the sixteenth NIC. Crowds of spectators and prospective investors were joined by a total of four thousand delegates from the United States, Mexico, Brazil, Chile, Germany, and South Africa. The auspicious Congress featured a variety of speeches and meetings, as well as parades, sporting events, parties and fireworks displays, all capped off by a lavish ball. "It was said to have been unequaled in the history of the Territory."[386]

That same year (1908), Ralph Twitchell was invited to participate in a conference on the conservation of the nation's resources that was being held at the White House. His friend, President Theodore Roosevelt, was calling together the country's governors along with roughly "140 picked students of American affairs to consider measures for the conservation of our country's great natural resources."[387] Preserving the remaining forests, safeguarding the public lands and waterways, and halting the rapacious consumption of resources was important to Roosevelt. The country's supplies of coal, oil, wood, and water were quickly being depleted; what remained was slipping into the clutches of a few wealthy individuals, and he was "determined to wrest the people's property alike from the ruthless hands of waste and from the greedy hands of monopoly."[388]

The event was totally unprecedented. "Never before in the history of the nation [had] a President conferred with the governors of the States."[389] Forty-two state governors made the trip to Washington D. C. for the meeting, along with five territorial governors and one ex-governor.[390] Each one brought along three, appointed "conferees representing colleges and commercial associations interested in the subjects of the conference and students of natural resources."[391] The governors of Arkansas, California and Massachusetts were unable to attend, but all three sent envoys. Twitchell accompanied Governor George Curry as a member of the New Mexico delegation.[392] Like so many times before, he was once again at the epicenter of a historical event. The assembly was the very first Conference of Governors, a function that has been repeated annually ever since.[393]

In 1909, the NIC convened its seventeenth session in Spokane, Washington, and Ralph Twitchell was present once again. He does not appear to have held a prominent position at this session, nor was he among the speakers listed in the program. Nevertheless, his influence within the NIC seems to have been at an all time high. Amid the proceedings he was elected first vice-president of the organization.[394]

In addition to being the first vice-president, Twitchell was heavily involved in spreading the message of the NIC via a so-called "missionary movement in behalf of the congress."[395] He traveled extensively across the West gaining support for irrigation, reclamation, and other conservation issues. He was also involved in organizing delegations from New Mexico for the eighteenth session of the NIC, which was slated for Pueblo, Colorado in 1910.[396]

At the Pueblo conference R. E. Twitchell was both the second highest-ranking officer in the congress and the head of the New Mexico delegation.[397] As such, he was instrumental in making New Mexico the star of the session. He had the territorial delegation operating so efficiently that they outshone everyone at the convention. According to Willard Holt of the Deming Graphic, "New Mexico was the 'whole thing' at the National Irrigation Congress in Pueblo."[398] His article boasted that attendees from across the country congratulated New Mexico's delegation on their superlative organization and boosting spirit. He also claimed that the New Mexicans "got everything [they] wanted except Twitchell for the presidency," and that New Mexico "did more advertising than all the rest of the delegations put together."[399]

By 1910 few Americans were more involved in irrigation and reclamation than R. E. Twitchell. He had done as much as anyone to promote water conservation issues in New Mexico, and "as first vice-president of the Congress he also contributed to the formulation of the reclamation policy adopted by the Nation."[400]

Beyond the 1910 session, records of Twitchell's affiliation with the NIC are spotty. There is a newspaper editorial from 1911 referring to him as "one of the most active and prominent members of the National Irrigation congress," but not much else for years.[401] Presumably, he continued to attend the NIC gatherings year after year, though his involvement in the organization obviously abated.

The NIC continued to meet until 1916, changing its name to the International Irrigation Congress in 1912. The only exception being the 1913 event, which was postponed because Phoenix was "unable to satisfy the executive committee of the congress that it was in a position to care for the big attendance."[402] In all likelihood, Twitchell was present at each conference; however, the only verifiable link between him and the group during that span indicates that he was a New Mexico delegate at the 22nd session, held in 1915.[403]

The abrupt shift in Ralph Twitchell's relationship with the congress was probably due to the advent of the Panama-California Exposition, a massive fair held in San Diego to commemorate the opening of the Panama Canal in 1915.[404] In 1910, Twitchell was named to the committee tasked with arranging a New Mexico exhibit for that event.[405] He then spent the next five years working tirelessly to ensure that New Mexico was well represented at San Diego. Indeed, "It was in the New Mexico Exhibit at the San Diego Exposition, ... that his genius for creating spectacular effects and for obtaining publicity, reached its apogee."[406]

When the New Mexico Exposition Commission mustered to begin making preparations for the expo there were no funds available to them. An air of apprehension permeated the assembly; however, the uncertainty, the lack of finances, and the timidity of many present did nothing to deter Twitchell. He forged ahead without hesitation. "He had a vision, a dream, and when he laid his plans before the Commission, they gasped at his daring."[407] Twitchell thought to construct in San Diego, a facsimile of the ancient Franciscan mission erected at the Acoma Pueblo in eastern New Mexico. The singularly attractive edifice would then be filled with innovative exhibits that were a far cry from the usual heaps of fruit and rocks that were generally offered up by counties and states at such events. He intended to incorporate cutting-edge cinematic technology, as well as a variety of other innovations, to enliven the displays. Not all of the commissioners whole-heartedly supported the idea, but Twitchell was able to convince enough of them that his plan was the prudent course. The New Mexico Exposition Commission chose the venerable old church as the model for the state's expo building and Twitchell as their leader, electing him president of the state's Board of Exposition Managers.[408]

Though financing was a question initially, the state eventually came through with two separate appropriations to cover the cost of erecting the building and manufacturing the exhibits. Contributions from private citizens and individual counties supplemented these funds.[409] Altogether, New Mexico spent nearly $20,000 constructing its building.[410] The Santa Fe based architectural partnership of I. H. and W. M. Rapp, was enlisted to execute the design. As per Twitchell's suggestion, the building Isaac Rapp conceptualized reflected the general lines of the San Esteban Mission at Acoma, though a few features of the San Felipe and Cochiti Pueblo missions were also incorporated.[411]

The intention was to make the building the embodiment of the "new-old Santa Fe style" of architecture, sometimes called Pueblo-Revival style, that had been taking shape in New Mexico's capital since roughly 1912. That year, this new architectural idiom was articulated as part of the "Plan of 1912," which "called for the consistent application of a motif incorporating adobe construction, portales, exposed vigas, canales, and other features of Pueblo and Spanish architecture."[412] Twitchell had long been identified with the movement, having constructed a home in Santa Fe along those lines in 1913. The Santa Fe New Mexican even credits him with having been "a moving spirit behind the Santa Fe Architectural idea."[413] In his conversations with Rapp, he had not just casually suggested what he thought the building should look like, he was pushing an agenda that involved designating Santa Fe as exotic and different, and he thought the building should be used to further that agenda, and serve as a structural advertisement for New Mexico.

In August 1912, Twitchell traveled to San Diego to personally select the site in Balboa Park where the New Mexico Building would be constructed. To ensure that as many people as possible would see the promotional edifice he chose "the most prominent location on the grounds, directly in front of the main building of the exposition."[414] New Mexico's faux tabernacle was to be unavoidable, the first thing visitors encountered upon entering the premises and the last thing they saw when leaving. With the site designated, construction was initiated.

The new architectural style coalescing in the form of New Mexico's expo building was fairly sparse in nature and relatively inexpensive to complete. This allowed for a majority of the allocated funds to go toward filling the structure with remarkable exhibits. The state's exposition commission spent almost $30,000 on their displays and to festoon the "Cathedral of the Desert" with paintings.[415]

New Mexico's building for the Panama-California Exposition at San Diego was completed in July 1914. Even before the grounds had been landscaped, the structure was attracting attention. Representatives of other states, drawn in by the rustic yet majestic edifice, found exhibits taking shape within that were radically different than the displays they were arranging. The New Mexicans were utilizing motion picture films, colored slides, models, and replicas in their exhibits. This novel approach caused a sensation, spurring several states to abandon their original plans in favor of exhibits modeled on the new New Mexico paradigm.[416]

A consummate micromanager, Twitchell was actively involved in arranging New Mexico's expo submission. In preparation for the event he put together his second comprehensive promotional volume showcasing New Mexico.[417] He also filmed a portion of the motion picture produced to highlight the state's many industries.[418] Working in conjunction with his close friend, Museum of New Mexico Director Edgar Hewett, he assembled items for a Spanish-colonial arts exhibit.[419] Additionally, when the various exhibit models and replicas were delivered to San Diego, he personally supervised the placing of the displays within the New Mexico building.[420]

New Mexico Governor William C. McDonald dedicated the state's expo building during the first week of May 1915. Hundreds gathered to witness the auspicious ceremony that included live music in addition to speeches. As the head of New Mexico's Exposition Commission Twitchell presided over the affair. He opened the proceedings with a characteristically modest address that focused solely on the inspiration for the building's design and "the high ideals to which the exposition commission had clung despite the voices that sought to lure it from the path of beauty and historic precedence."[421] As if to reinforce the connection between New Mexico and the United States, he described the architecture as distinctly American, a product of the hybrid cultural composition of the continent. With that, he presented the building to the governor, who accepted on behalf of the state, calling the building "an embodiment of the spirit of the commonwealth, of its traditions, its history, its ideals."[422] McDonald also had hearty words of praise for Twitchell, marveling at his inexhaustible energy and commending his enthusiasm and zeal. Every speaker that followed also paid tribute to Twitchell, recognizing him as the individual most responsible for the structure and the exhibits contained within.[423]

R. E. Twitchell at Las Vegas, New Mexico, July 4, 1914. Photographer: Waldo Twitchell.
Courtesy of the Palace of the Governors Photo Archives (NMHM/DCA), #054276

In addition to being esthetically beautiful, the New Mexico building was also extremely large, which served to benefit the state because throughout the yearlong festivities their reception hall was used to host many of the exposition's marquee events.[424] Most notable among these was the "Roosevelt Day" celebration honoring former president Theodore Roosevelt. The revered dignitary actually attended the event, making for a particularly momentous occasion. After arriving at the grounds under military escort, the legendary gentleman-roughneck was greeted by the directors of the exposition before being spirited to the New Mexico building where a crowd of invited guests had gathered. Stepping from the automobile, Roosevelt immediately spotted Twitchell, who had been waiting to receive him. Shunting everyone else aside, the former president proceeded directly to his old friend with arms outstretched and exclaimed, "Well, Colonel, I am certainly glad to see you again."[425] With a hearty handshake the two strode into the "Cathedral of the Desert" arm and arm, while those assembled cheered wildly. The program of events for "Roosevelt Day" included music and a slide-show featuring pictures of the notorious Rough Riders, as well as a tour of New Mexico's avant-garde exhibits. By all accounts Roosevelt had a wonderful time and was delighted with all he saw. He too offered up words of praise for Twitchell, crediting his friend with helping to make New Mexico a highlight of the expo.[426]

Ralph Twitchell "saw to it that New Mexico was not only worthily represented but 'led all the rest,' at the Panama-California Exposition."[427] The state's building was the premier attraction. Hundreds of visitors piled into the artful faux-adobe hall day after day to see the films and marvel at the exhibits.[428] A variety of magazines and newspapers ran features on the structure, giving the state thousands of dollars worth of free publicity.[429] All told, New Mexico received five awards for their submission, including the prize for The Best State Exhibit.[430] Defying convention, Twitchell had set a new standard of excellence in American expositions. In the process he also helped usher in a new era in advertising, as he was one of the first people to promote a state using motion pictures.[431]

Despite the impressive showing, not everyone in New Mexico was happy with Twitchell. The Pueblo Indians from Taos were upset with him and the rest of the exposition commission because a surreptitiously filmed recording of their Fiesta de San Geronimo was included in the stream of films shown in the state's expo building. When Twitchell and his crew had inquired about shooting the rite, the Pueblos had expressly forbade it, but a sly camera operator managed to capture footage of the ritual anyway, by covering his camera lens with a tin can he had punched a hole through. The arcane observance included a dance that was never performed for the general public, and the Pueblos were outraged when they discovered the ceremony had been filmed and was being exhibited. They claimed that a spate of spiritual disharmony within their village was due to the public exhibition of the film. The Pueblos wanted the footage destroyed. Some of Twitchell's Indian friends even told him that they would do away with the film if given the opportunity.[432]

Twitchell evidently had no compunctions about running the film, however. He continued to show the reels until one afternoon late in July 1915 they were stolen from New Mexico's expo building. While the structure stood empty that summer day, someone broke in and purloined the film. When Twitchell returned to his office in the early evening he discovered a window had been forced open, a strongbox had been rifled, and the room housing the films had been looted. He also found an explanation scrawled on a piece of paper in broken English. The note read: "Bad mediceen—indians have bad luck—all sick. Pichers of race must burn—indians all get well."[433] The San Diego Union attributed the theft to Native Americans, and that certainly makes sense given the circumstances, but the culprits were never apprehended.[434]

Ever resourceful, Twitchell capitalized on the publicity, using the incident to promote New Mexico's presence at the expo. He also had a duplicate of the unsanctioned film shipped to him from Santa Fe. This undoubtedly compounded the effrontery to the Taos Pueblos, but Twitchell appears to have completely disregarded their feelings. Clearly, the only thing that mattered to him was the ascendancy of New Mexico to national prominence.[435]

Deemed worthy of saving, the iconic New Mexico Building was maintained by the Balboa Park Board after the conclusion of the expo. They intended to make the distinctive edifice part of the Art and Archaeological Museum.[436] In 1917, San Diego bought the building from New Mexico, and kept the structure intact until 1935 when it was redesigned at the behest of officials of the California Pacific International Exposition, who wanted to use it as a state of California Palace of Education.[437]

The "Cathedral of the Desert" was so well received at the Panama-California Expo that a faction of New Mexicans came to believe it should be "brought home" and reproduced in the state capital.[438] Among them was Twitchell, who was of the opinion that the building should be re-created in Santa Fe for use as a new state museum. As a regent of the Museum of New Mexico, he was aware that that organization was having issues with the availability of space in the Palace of the Governors where they generally exhibited their collections, so he approached the museum's founder and director, Edgar Hewett, about using the expo building as a model for a new museum.[439] The idea proved popular, and on March 1, 1915 the state House of Representatives approved a bill allocating $30,000 to help fund the project. This figure was eventually matched by donations from private citizens. In 1917 the building was completed on the northwest corner of the plaza in Santa Fe.[440] Known today as the Fine Arts Museum, the structure still stands in the heart of the city.

At the Panama-California Exposition, New Mexico and its capital were the beneficiaries of "advertising such as few states or cities have ever received."[441] The exposure went a long way toward undermining the prevailing view of the state as a wild, dangerous hinterland populated by foreigners. For his part, Twitchell received a great deal of acclaim. He was widely considered New Mexico's greatest proponent, a sentiment that was artfully articulated in April 1916 by a member of the Santa Fe Chamber of Commerce named Frank Owen. In a speech nominating Twitchell for the chamber's presidency, Owen described him as the "Chief of all Boostmasters."[442]

The image of New Mexico as a bounteous utopia that Twitchell broadcast to the world at events like the sixteenth National Irrigation Congress and the Panama-California Exposition changed many people's perception of the state. For instance, approximately half of the people who visited New Mexico's Expo Building in San Diego did not know the difference between the state and the Republic of Mexico.[443] Filing through the "Cathedral of the desert" served to clear up that little misunderstanding, and left many visitors with a new sense of their country, its southwestern expanses defined in their minds for the first time. For thousands of Americans, New Mexico went from foreign to familiar, and the idea of traveling there no longer seemed dangerous and absurd.

The tourist industry that Twitchell and others had been actively fostering since 1912 began to materialize. With the commencement of the Fiesta de Santa Fe in 1920, New Mexico's capital became one of the premiere tourist destinations in the western hemisphere. Throughout the 1920s, gadabouts from across the country made their way to New Mexico. Trains still conveyed a share of these

travelers, but many opted to make the trip in automobiles, an increasingly popular means of transportation. This onslaught of motorists rolled across the state
on easily traversable roads that traced back to Twitchell. New Mexico's highway
system was capable of handling the increasing numbers of automotive tourists
because constructing a network of roads had long been an objective of the state's
boosters, Twitchell chief among them.

Highways channeling travelers into the heart of New Mexico were integral
to the success of his plans for Santa Fe and the rest of the state, so he worked
hard to gather support for building roads. He has been credited with calling
New Mexico's first road congress.[444a] Moreover, he served as president of the
New Mexico branch of two different national road-building organizations, the
"Good Roads" Association and the National Highways Association.[444b, 444c] He
regularly toured the state lecturing on the importance of quality roads.

9

Omnibus

"We are told we are dreamers, but I want to say that it was a dreamer of dreams, the enthusiast, the sentimentalist who has ever accomplished great things described on the pages of history."
—Ralph Emerson Twitchell[445]

Much like his namesake, Ralph Waldo Emerson, Ralph Twitchell was a prolific writer. He primarily wrote histories relating to New Mexico. Over a span of roughly four decades he authored a variety of historical monographs, textbooks, magazine articles, lectures, an extensive family genealogy, and even a hit song. He also founded his own historical magazine. In addition to being a gifted writer, Twitchell was also a skilled archivist and was responsible for preserving a collection of priceless documents from New Mexico's time as a Spanish colony.

An avid chronicler with a knack for assaying written material, compiling details, and recapitulating information, Twitchell achieved no small amount of fame as the foremost expert in New Mexico history. His masterwork, a multi-volume history of New Mexico entitled The Leading Facts of New Mexico History, was recognized as the definitive work in the field for decades and is still considered a literary classic. Simply stated, Twitchell articulated the idea of New Mexico for generations of Americans because his accounts of the region's past colored the way the state was perceived. All things considered, Twitchell's writings constitute perhaps his most significant contribution to posterity.

Twitchell developed an interest in New Mexico's past shortly after his arrival in the territory in 1883. A chance encounter with the great historian and archaeologist Adolph Bandolier, who was in Santa Fe conducting research on the Southwest, sparked his curiosity.[446] The two cultivated a friendship and for a time Twitchell was a pupil of the elder scholar.[447] Bandolier was delving into the archival remnants of the Spanish occupation period housed by the territorial government. The Swiss ethnographer's enthusiasm for the material proved infectious; his young protégé developed a keen interest in the brittle old documents. Twitchell began studying the ancient papers closely, spending "hours digging deeply into the archival resources, discovering fascinating bits of history long buried."[448]

Beyond his annalistic passions and interest in the Spanish occupation period, "Twitchell saw an affinity between the legal profession and the study of history, particularly research in documentary sources."[449] He believed that proficiency in both fields depended upon a particular set of skills, the research and writing done in historiography being analogous to the way an attorney prepares for a case. He also identified similarities in the way facts and events are presented in the courtroom and on the page. As far as he was concerned, they were all but one and the same. In reference to historiography he once said, "the historical writer should not be merely a narrator, chronicler. He should not be the witness giving testimony. He should be the lawyer, the advocate, the painter, the artist evolving an historical picture for the mind and creating impressions which result in conclusions."[450]

By February 1884, Twitchell had decided to try his hand as a writer. On Valentine's Day of that year he told a newspaper reporter, "I care not who makes the valentines, so I can write the fables."[451] His first significant offering was not completed for another seven years, but with his workload as an attorney, political figure, and promoter he had very little time left for writing. He stole moments when he could though, and there were even times when his interest in history took precedence over his political duties and his obligations to his employer.[452]

In 1891, Ralph Emerson Twitchell became a published book author. He was vice-president of the state bar association and a member of its Committee on the History of the Bench and Bar of New Mexico. This committee had been tasked with compiling a history of the New Mexico Bench and Bar during the early years of American governance, and Twitchell did not shy away from the opportunity to author such a historically significant piece. Tackling the subject with his characteristic verve he constructed a twenty page record of the period that was published under the title *The Bench and Bar of New Mexico During the American Occupation, A.D. 1846–1850.*[453]

The literary offering was accompanied by a lecture he gave before the bar association covering the distinguished lawyers that "occupied places of prominence" in New Mexico history, "beginning with the first Judicial officers named by Gen. Kearney in 1846."[454] The masterly address "elicited the encomiums of all present," leading the Santa Fe Daily New Mexican to rave, "the young barrister certainly did himself proud."[455]

Though nearly two decades passed before Twitchell published another work, he was always involved in a literary endeavor of some kind. Notably, he continued to write speeches and to lecture, and crafted artful addresses that lent to his fame as "one of the most eloquent speakers of the Southwest."[456] Although many of his disquisitions dealt with aspects of New Mexico history, he was comfortable perorating on any number of subjects. In 1897, he was called upon to address the annual gathering of the New Mexico Horticultural Association, and a year later he was speaking before a crowd in Las Vegas, gathered in celebration of an American military victory in the Spanish-American War. Two months after that, in September 1898, he delivered a speech honoring the state's volunteer soldiers, the newly canonized Rough Riders, during a Peace Jubilee in Albuquerque.[457] The following year, he spoke at the Raton High School commencement about the virtues of public education.[458] Glowing reviews of Twitchell's orations led to greater and greater demand for his services, while his "sonorous voice and a gift for emphasizing the human interest in history, assured him rapt attention and applause whenever he spoke in public."[459] A couple of his most favorably received lectures were repeated multiple times to sizable audiences.[460]

Whenever his schedule permitted, Twitchell returned time and again to the archival remnants of the Spanish occupation that he first investigated with Adolph Bandolier. Ensorcelled by the region's history, particularly the European invasion, he spent long hours pouring over the collection of archaic memoranda tracing the exploits of trespassing Iberians. "He had an almost proprietary attitude toward these archives."[461] Considering the collection a priceless vestige of the region's past, he was literally willing to risk his life to protect it. Housed in the territorial capital building in Santa Fe, the cache of documents was generally well guarded from harm, but when the structure caught fire on May 12, 1892, the precious trove was imperiled. Responding without hesitation, "Twitchell rushed to the scene where he enlisted several bystanders, and together they fought their way through the smoke to the room holding the archives."[462] With the precious files in hand the contingent fled the rising conflagration, and escaped with all of the invaluable documents as the building incinerated. Twitchell's quick thinking and wanton disregard for his own welfare, as well as that of his neighbors, saved the irreplaceable compilation of writings from certain destruction. Shortly after the rescuers emerged from the flames the edifice was reduced to ash and all the contemporary records still inside were lost.[463]

Extricating the Spanish Archives from the inferno made Twitchell even more possessive of them. He assumed responsibility for stewardship of the treasured pages, and publicized details of thievery and looting by document hunters, and even went so far as to expose where a few of the stolen articles lay hidden. When he located valuable materials tucked away in private collections, he selflessly expended his own resources to purchase the items, acquiring them for the archive without thinking twice about the cost. Therefore, he was understandably upset when a portion of the collection was removed to the Library of Congress in 1903. He protested the removal of the records, but to no avail. His position as the unofficial steward of the stockpile did not entitle him to as much as a vote on the matter. Without recourse, he could only watch as the collection he prized was plundered in the interests of the national library.[464]

The Spanish Archives featured prominently in Twitchell's writings, and indeed constituted one of his many literary works. He carefully translated and transcribed the documents, compiling the information into two volumes. In 1914, the pair was published as The Spanish Archives of New Mexico. The books were exhaustively annotated and beautifully illustrated. They were also well received by the paramount expert in the field. "Dr. F. W. Hodge, director of the bureau of ethnology in Washington," who was considered "the leading authority in the United States on southwestern history," had high praise for the offering.[465] He thought the arrangement of the documents "excellent," and described the annotations as "all that a work of the kind demands."[466] Dr. Hodge also said the work would "prove of the utmost value to students," and congratulated both Twitchell on his tremendous achievement and New Mexico for "the wisdom of its selection of compiler and editor."[467] After assessing the work as "well worth while," he added that it would be inestimably valuable to him personally, because it provided him with material he had long sought.[468]

Though Twitchell conducted the work on the archives for the state of New Mexico, he did so without receiving monetary compensation and at considerable personal expense. He may have believed he would recover his costs out of the proceeds from the sale of the books. If that was the case, however, it was a gross overestimation of the public demand for the work. Not a single copy of The Spanish Archives of New Mexico sold in 1914.[469]

The lack of interest in these volumes may have surprised Twitchell. He had authored several other books prior to publishing the archival material and probably expected a warmer response. His first public offering, The History of the Military Occupation of the Territory of New Mexico from 1846 to 1851 by the Government of the United States, published in 1909, was "a landmark book on General Stephen W. Kearny's conquest of the territory."[470] The Rio Grande Republican declared it "a monumental work" and "a notable contribution to literature" while the first editions were still on the press.[471]

Ralph Emerson Twitchell, 1910? Photograph Courtesy of the Palace of the Governors (MNM/DCA), #007902

Two years later, Twitchell followed The History of the Military Occupation of the Territory of New Mexico with the first volume of his masterwork, The Leading Facts of New Mexico History, a comprehensive history of the region he had been working on for more than a quarter of a century. This book inspired so much confidence that a whopping fifteen hundred copies were printed in 1911, which The Santa Fe New Mexican took as an indication that The Leading Facts was bound "to be the greatest achievement, historically speaking, in the annals of southwestern records."[472] While a bit hyperbolic, this assessment turned out to be fairly accurate. The five-volume Leading Facts of New Mexico History was considered the authoritative chronicle of the southwest for generations and was Twitchell's most renowned publication.[473]

Volume one of Leading Facts was largely a recounting of the Spanish occupation period that Twitchell pieced together using smoke-tinged documents from the Spanish Archives.[474] His own library provided supplemental source material, as did the libraries of his friends L. Bradford Prince and Thomas Catron. He relied on these private collections all throughout the process of bringing The Leading Facts to five massive volumes.[475] When he found that the work he had undertaken could not be completed without consulting archival resources outside of New Mexico, he lit out across the globe. His research took him "from almost every pre-historic ruin in the state to the official archives of Madrid, Mexico and Washington, and from the kiva where the historic legends of the Pueblo Indian are transmitted, to the vaults where the sacred records of the Franciscan fathers are kept at Rome."[476] The second volume in the series, published in 1912, covered the Mexican era up through the American takeover and into modern times, including the advent of statehood.[477] These first two volumes alone were a monumental historical achievement that was made even greater by the publication of three further installments in 1917. This trio dealt with the histories of individual counties and the early years of statehood.[478] All together, the five volumes of this exhaustive historical classic tip the scales at nearly twenty pounds.[479]

In the early twentieth century, few states, if any, had been so thoroughly studied and written about by one individual. Twitchell's work set a new precedent. Not only was he "a pioneer investigator," but also his Leading Facts "is so painstakingly complete that while it may be modified or enlarged it will never be superseded."[480] The Farmington Enterprise once avowed a belief that these books contained "about all the facts from the sixteenth to the twentieth century that it will ever be possible to collect."[481] Although that was a bit of a stretch, Twitchell's Leading Facts was the most significant historical work on the Southwest published in the first half of the twentieth century. Eight years after publication of the final volume, The Albuquerque Morning Journal likened the entire series to The History of the Decline and Fall of the Roman Empire, calling it the supreme American state history.[482]

Authorship of The Leading Facts of New Mexico History made Twitchell the state's resident history expert. Indeed, he was honored as such in 1914, when he "was made official state historian by a legislative act."[483] The same year he received this appointment he also published a textbook that he had coauthored with another scholar. Fittingly, the man whose name had become synonymous with New Mexico history also had a hand in writing the history book that would be used to educate the state's school children. His partner in the endeavor was Dr. Frank H. H. Roberts. Their collaboration yielded a combination civics and history textbook that was adopted in 1914 as the official book "for the higher grades of the public schools."[484] To keep students' costs low both authors worked without pay.[485]

Ralph Twitchell's historiographic endeavors at this time also included editing the historical quarterly Old Santa Fe, which he founded in 1913. "He took great pride in his labor of love as editor of this historical magazine whose fame as the most interesting publication of that kind, brought him in touch with historical research workers and writers the world over."[486] Beyond his responsibilities as editor, Twitchell was the periodical's leading contributor.[487] Articles written by his second wife Estelle Bennett Burton were also regular features.[488] Old Santa Fe remained in publication for three years, operating from 1913 to 1916.[489]

After Old Santa Fe was discontinued, Twitchell found other outlets to publish his historical musings. In September 1916, he furnished National Geographic with an article he had written about Santa Fe.[490] Later, a submission of his appeared in a Chicago based publication ironically named The Santa Fe Magazine.[491] He also published numerous historical monographs through the School of American Research and the New Mexico Historical Society.[492] Between 1917 and 1925, he was responsible for composing eight of the eleven bulletins published by the society. He also cataloged their extensive collections. This work, along with several other papers he had written were "either ready for the press or nearly so," when illness overtook him.[493]

The last of Twitchell's books were also awaiting publication when he was hospitalized in 1925. His final public offering, entitled The Story of Old Santa Fe, was being readied for issue while he clung to life.[494] It was "a study which oriented the story of New Mexico around developments within the 300-year old capital."[495] Unfortunately, Twitchell did not live to see a single copy in a bookseller's display case. He did, however, have a chance to glimpse the finished product. An advance proof of the text was presented to him as he lay on his deathbed. This tangible representation of the legacy he was leaving behind may have provided some comfort during his last days. Copies of this crowning work were coming off the presses of the New Mexico Publishing Corporation as the famed author passed away.[496]

His terminal work was published posthumously. Shortly before he died, Twitchell finished editing an extensive family genealogy he had spent years compiling.[497] This was "his most laborious and most painstaking work."[498] When he initiated the project his intention had been to incorporate the names of every Twitchell in the country. He fell short of that overly ambitious goal, but his efforts were still wildly successful. His book included every ancestor and relative he could track down. The typescript was entrusted to the family after his death. Included in the papers was an invitation to future generations to make changes and additions.[499] Herbert Kenaston Twitchell, the author's second cousin, gladly shouldered the financial responsibility for having the roughly seven hundred pages printed and bound. He too ended up dying before the work was published, however, and it was his widow, Mary Adelaide Twitchell, who saw the project through.[500]

No accounting of Ralph Twitchell's literary accomplishments would be complete without mentioning his proficiency as a songwriter. In 1919, he collaborated with a well-known composer named Arthur Fournier to create a song about New Mexico's ancient capital, entitled "Old Santa Fe."[501] The ballad became a radio hit across the country and a beloved anthem in Santa Fe, where it was still available for purchase thirty years after being written.[502]

On top of his short, yet wildly successful music career, Twitchell was also "the most prolific New Mexico historian of his period."[503] His descriptions of the state and its past helped shape Americans' views of the southwest for at least a quarter of a century. Quite frankly, he authored historical classics. They were hardly perfect, however. Some of Twitchell's translations were faulty, and many of his interpretations and deductions were proven to be inadequate or wrong by later historians. Additionally, his assessments were not always completely objective. Though he did his best to judge his contemporaries fairly, his "treatment of the territorial and early statehood periods was influenced by his own interests, convictions, and political commitments."[504]

For obvious reasons, Twitchell was prone to applying "the whitewash brush" when enumerating the exploits of his political allies.[505] He was also not above relegating his adversaries to obscurity, as he did with Democratic governor Edmund G. Ross. However, his motivation for treating Governor Ross with utter disregard had nothing to do with the latter's reform agenda as has been suggested.[506] Recall the fact that Governor Ross had been responsible for the shady dealings concerning the Office of Solicitor General in 1883, which had ultimately led to Twitchell's refusal to ever hold another elected office. By ignoring Governor Ross he was not shortchanging a political disputant, the omission was personal and vengeful, the final blow in a decades old conflict.

Twitchell's shortcomings as a historian bespoke his lack of formal training, as well as his personal investment in the territory/state. They have been pointed out by ensuing generations of professional historians as evidence of the inadequacies, errors, and biases in his work. That having been said, Twitchell's critics often failed to recognize the context of the era within which these ambitious, pioneering histories were written.[507]

The literary works of Ralph Twitchell were neither the first nor the last histories written about New Mexico, but they were a significant advancement in that progression. While critically flawed by modern historiographical standards, his books were not without merit. A majority of the information contained therein was valid, if somewhat colored by the author's personal and political inclinations. In spite of their perceived subjectivity, Twitchell's works contributed greatly to the advancement of southwestern historiography. Beyond raising the bar for historical literature, his volumes provided a valuable frame of reference for more qualified professionals to utilize thereafter. Later historians had the benefit of his perspective on events, and in some instances the added benefit of firsthand knowledge he had acquired over the course of a life spanning several of the most eventful decades in New Mexico history. More than just a historian, he was also an eyewitness and at times a participant in the exploits he recounted on the pages of his tomes. This alone makes his texts undeniably important as primary source materials.

Of the many meaningful contributions Ralph Twitchell made to the field of historiography in the Southwest, one stands out as his most consequential and enduring. The books he authored ensured that his name would be affiliated with New Mexico in perpetuity, but all his writings paled in importance next to the historical significance of preserving the Spanish Archives. Protecting these priceless, one of a kind documents and safeguarding them for future specialists to analyze had far-reaching implications. In a very tangible way, Twitchell's archival work and vigilance as a warder made all the subsequent scholarship involving these papers possible. Every insight into the past that these records provided came courtesy of his soot-streaked hands.[508]

10

The End of the Line

"It is not length of life, but depth of life."
—Ralph Waldo Emerson

Ralph Emerson Twitchell lived for just sixty-six years, but his life was fuller than most. The passion and industry with which he approached every undertaking was admirable, but it was also incredible. His friends marveled at his boundless energy, and were amazed that he actually had time for avocational pursuits like writing when his dance card was always full.[509] Yet, he did manage to make time for writing and a whole lot more. Even in his declining years he was more productive than many men in the prime of their lives. Only after illness forced his hand did he step away from his exceedingly busy schedule. Unfortunately, first-rate medical attention and months of bed rest were not enough to restore his failing health, and after a long, sapping fight he finally succumbed. Upon hearing of his death nearly all of New Mexico and many others around the globe mourned the loss. Tragically, Twitchell's early demise probably could have been prevented had he been able to subjugate his indomitable personality and abide by the recommendations of his physicians.

In April 1925, Ralph Twitchell was forced to undergo an unspecified surgery at St. Vincent's hospital in Santa Fe.[510] After his condition failed to improve postoperatively, a second procedure followed. Initially, this subsequent operation appeared to be successful, but soon thereafter complications arose, and Twitchell was again confined to a bed. Following the two surgical procedures his life hung "in the balance for months but his intense vitality stood him in good stead."[511]

By far the biggest challenge Twitchell faced as a patient was keeping his mind occupied during his confinement. He had a hard time tolerating the countless hours being wasted while he lay indisposed. For someone used to having many fish to fry, this was an intense personal trial. In fact, he was so eager to return to his myriad affairs he may have actually compromised his own rehabilitation. His drive and vigor, which had compelled him to strive for perfection in every walk of life, had become a detriment to his health, and he had to be forcibly deterred from resuming his labors while still in recovery.[512]

Confined to a bed with nothing to occupy himself, Twitchell grew despondent. The precipitous drop in his morale alarmed many of those around him who worried what effects it might have on his recuperation. Indeed, there was cause for concern; his convalescence lagged behind expectations. When he failed to regain his health in the time frame allotted by his doctors, the decision was made to have him transported to Los Angeles for further treatment.[513] The low altitude on the coast was deemed more salubrious, and the skilled medical professionals in California better equipped to deal with iatrical crises.[514] His son Waldo was residing in Los Angeles at that time as well, and that also may have factored into the decision to move the ailing Twitchell.[515]

On June 24, 1925 Twitchell was hurriedly conveyed to Clara Barton Hospital in Los Angeles. Along the way his constitution began to flag and those attending him diagnosed his symptoms as being consistent with uremic poisoning. The situation appeared dire, and were it not for the "strenuous emergency measures" undertaken by his physicians, he surely would have perished on that summer day.[516]

Once comfortably installed in Southern California, there was an immediate improvement in Twitchell's condition. His disease-ravaged body rallied and "it was believed the poison had been eliminated."[517] He was not yet out of the woods, but the upswing in his health was accompanied by a corresponding lift in his spirits that gave everyone involved reason to hope for the best. After weeks of dejected misery on account of his forced inactivity, Twitchell's depression seemingly melted away. Perhaps, just being in the presence of his beloved son Waldo had been enough to drag him out of his doldrums.[518]

Twitchell appeared to be on the mend. His strength returned and for a time he looked as if he would recover fully. This amelioration only served to compound his restlessness, however. The company of his son had been a much-needed tonic, but he missed his work and the companionship of his friends in Santa Fe. He hated being so disconnected from events in New Mexico, and the many letters he received from his comrades while laid up in the hospital "were a great source of consolation in the loneliness of a man accustomed to plunging into every kind of public activity."[519]

By no means an easy patient, Twitchell micromanaged his own care, often disagreeing with the recommendations of his doctors. Inexplicably, he refused medication and treatment at times, "determined to get well his way or not at all."[520] He became enraged whenever he was not allowed to control his rehabilitation. As a result, his convalescence was repeatedly undermined by sinking spells that sapped his energy and left him thoroughly enfeebled. Eventually, his wife and son were told to stop visiting his bedside because of the wild tantrums he threw in their presence; he was absolutely convinced they were "killing him by not agreeing with him."[521]

During the last week of July, Ralph Twitchell's condition regressed significantly and he was again at death's door. His collapse came on abruptly, shortly after his wife's departure for Santa Fe, where she intended to tie up some affairs. Fearing that his father might perish before her return, Waldo telegraphed to intercept her along the way, in Barstow. Met with the unwelcome cable, Mrs. Twitchell rushed back to the hospital where she found her husband hanging on to life, though just barely.[522]

Much to everyone's surprise Twitchell rebounded yet again. Unfortunately, as his health improved he continued to insist on controlling his own remedial therapy. This need to call the shots bordered on mania. After a week, his strength had increased, but he was never really out of danger. Writing to family friend Lansing Bloom in early August, Waldo explained that his father's heart was "very bad," and that he was at risk of dying at any moment even though he was no longer facing any immediate danger.[523]

The second week of August brought further improvement in Twitchell's physical condition, as well as an ostensible change in his deportment. His combativeness abated, he held his temper in check, and he fully acquiesced to his doctor's orders. Having recognized how futile his efforts to influence the course of his treatment had become, he opted for sullen silence instead. He still seethed, however, angry not only with his medical practitioners but also with his son, who he was convinced was partly to blame for his current predicament because he would "not agree with him and order the nurses and doctors to do his bidding."[524] As a result, Waldo was forced to keep at a distance from his ailing father.[525]

After months of miserable torment at the hands of a still unexplained affliction Twitchell was finally stable. His wound was closed, his pulse was strong, and he was no longer suffering from fevers. His once imposing physique had been reduced to "skin and bones," but he retained "an amazing amount of physical strength."[526] He could raise himself and turnover in bed, and was loath to accept help with anything. According to Waldo, he was not in any pain. Mentally, his faculties remained entirely intact, although at times he had some difficulty concentrating. All appearances indicated he was persevering.[527]

With her husband apparently out of danger, Mrs. Twitchell was able to return to Santa Fe and initiate the process of relocating their household to California.[528] While she was away, however, the patient took a turn for the worse. On August 25, Waldo sent word that his father had sustained "a grave relapse and paralytic stroke."[529] She hurriedly left for Los Angeles.[530]

As darkness fell on the twenty-fifth, Ralph Emerson Twitchell lay close to death. His son sat with him, the two no longer at odds over anything. His wife was still en route, speeding west across the desert, hoping he would pull through like he had so many times before. Afraid the end was near, Waldo stood vigil by his father's side into the early morning hours of August 26, 1925. At 5:45, as the sky was beginning to fade into blue, Ralph Twitchell finally, peacefully succumbed. Mrs. Twitchell had not yet arrived.[531]

Word of Ralph Twitchell's death reached his friends and colleagues in New Mexico later that morning. Waldo wired the sorrowful news to The Santa Fe New Mexican. Included in his communiqué was the statement, "I feel Father belongs to Santa Fe and [I] am arranging for burial there."[532] During his final hours R. E. Twitchell had revealed to his son that he wished to be buried underneath The Cross of the Martyrs, the monolithic monument he had been instrumental in erecting on a knoll overlooking Santa Fe.[533] Not being the city's mayor, Waldo was not in a position to grant such a request, but he did what he could. He informed the Santa Fe City Council of the request, and they proved remarkably receptive to the idea, springing into action almost immediately. Swept up in the emotion of the moment, the council called a special meeting the following day to approve the revered figure's interment in the unorthodox locale.[534] The session lasted just long enough for the council to return a unanimous vote granting permission for his burial below the shrine.[535]

On August 27, 1925 Twitchell's remains departed Los Angeles for New Mexico aboard Santa Fe train number 2. His widow and son accompanied the body. The funeral was planned for three days hence, with burial "near the Cross of the Martyrs on the Heights of Cuma, north of Santa Fe."[536] The locomotive bearing his body arrived at Lamy, New Mexico on the evening of the twenty-eighth. A party of mourners assembled at the station to receive the bereaved. Among those gathered was the composer Arthur Fournier, who had written a song with the deceased seven years earlier.[537] As Twitchell rode into Santa Fe for the last time the flags above the Palace of the Governors and the State Museum stood at half-mast in solemn tribute.[538]

Funeral services for Colonel Ralph E. Twitchell took place at the Episcopal Church on Sunday, August 30, 1925. His body lay in state at his magnificent home on Grant Avenue from ten in the morning until noon.[539] Shortly before three o'clock his body was conveyed to the Church of the Holy Faith trailing "a cortege of autos half a mile long."[540] The procession of mourners was one of the longest in the city's history. All told, fifty automobiles escorted the casket through Santa Fe. At three o'clock, Reverend W. S. Trowbridge, the church rector, initiated the services. The requiem was simple yet impressive, if remarkably brief. Few words were spoken; the choir sang a brace of hymns. Still, "it was apparent that here was a demonstration of genuine mourning for the loss of a real friend."[541]

Twitchell's grieving friends included an assortment of New Mexico's Democrats and Republicans, as well as Protestants, Catholics, and Jews. Some had Anglo-Saxon forbears; others were of Spanish lineage. There were gentlemen "prominent in political and business circles, men and women who...attained eminence through their writing, painting and archaeological researches, and hundreds of men and women in the ordinary walks of life, some rich, many poor, all of whom had admired Colonel Twitchell and prized his friendship."[542] Nearly every part of New Mexico was represented.[543]

The famous painter Gerald Cassidy was one of six men who served as pallbearers. The other five included W. C. Reid, solicitor of the A. T. & S. F. Railroad; "R. L. Ormsbee, Chief Clerk of the penitentiary; Clinton J. Crandall, Superintendent of the Northern Pueblos; Wesley O. Conner, Superintendent of the State School for the Deaf and Dumb;" and R. F. Asplund, who directed the New Mexico Taxpayers Association.[544] The list of honorary pallbearers extended to thirty-one names and included the sitting mayor as well as a former one, a state senator, a couple of judges, an ex-governor, a former U. S. senator, and a host of other highly respected political figures and distinguished professionals.[545]

Preparations for Twitchell's interment below the Cross of the Martyrs had not been completed by the time of the funeral, so plans were made to have him temporarily buried in Fairview Cemetery. At the gravesite, a Masonic rite was preformed, Twitchell having been an initiate. Then Reverend Trowbridge closed the proceedings with the "Episcopal committal service."[546] When he had finished, the coffin, replete with "a profusion of flowers," was lowered into the arenaceous New Mexico soil.[547]

Epilogue

The death of Ralph Emerson Twitchell had a profound effect on many Santa Feans. In the days after his funeral the city remained awash in grief, with citizens wondering if something should be done to commemorate the life of a man who had accomplished so much on behalf of the city and state. At the regular session of the Santa Fe City Council, held on the first of September, the discourse revolved around honoring Twitchell for his numberless contributions to the community. That night the council passed a resolution urging Santa Feans "to join in a movement to erect a suitable memorial to Col. Ralph E. Twitchell, a monument worthy of his memory and of the city he so loved."[548] Included in the resolution was a stirring tribute that described Twitchell as a paragon of civic responsibility and public spirit. Residents were called upon to follow the example set by Twitchell and make Santa Fe "the noble city that he saw in his vision."[549]

Two weeks later, the monthly meeting of the New Mexico Historical Society convened within the Palace of the Governors. The September session was devoted entirely to memorializing Twitchell, who had been president of the organization. It was an informal affair, open to the public, consisting of short addresses given by several of Twitchell's closest friends. The proceedings began with onetime Attorney General Frank Clancy, one of the honorary pallbearers at the funeral, speaking about his friend's prowess as an attorney. He was followed by Lansing Bloom, the society's treasurer and secretary, who delivered a lecture on Twitchell as a historian. Next, attorney Edgar L. Street, another honorary pallbearer, gave a speech covering the work R. E. Twitchell did as a civil servant. Then Edgar Hewett, chief administrator of the Museum of New Mexico, talked about the honoree's connection to that organization. He too had served as an honorary pallbearer. At the end of the evening, artist Gerald Cassidy, who had been among those selected to actually carry Twitchell's casket, spoke of the deceased as a patron of the arts. He also submitted designs for a commemorative monument.[550]

Cassidy had painted a portrait of Twitchell some years earlier that had "attracted admiring attention" while being exhibited in the gallery of the state museum in 1924.[551] Another painting may have been what the artist had in mind for the memorial. Unfortunately, records do not clearly describe what the Historical Society commissioned as a tribute, and the piece has since disappeared.

Objections were raised regarding the relocation of Twitchell's coffin to the spot he had designated beneath the cross, so his remains were left in Fairview cemetery.[552] This was probably for the best; Santa Fe grew significantly after 1925 and houses now surround the giant concrete crucifix. Thus, his body would have had to be moved from that location at some point anyway.

Despite the enthusiastic support for fashioning a cenotaph dedicated to Twitchell, no suitable monument appears to have been erected by the city. A plaque by the martyr's cross bears his name, but only relates his connection to that massive cruciate, telling nothing of his other exploits. Strangely his name appears nowhere else in Santa Fe. While streets downtown bear names like Nusbaum, Otero, Catron, and Prince, Twitchell is noticeably absent.

There was a Twitchell Street in Santa Fe at one time; it lay just north of the plaza. In the early twentieth century what is today East Marcy Street was called Twitchell Street. However, by 1913 the name had fallen out of use and the thoroughfare became known as Marcy Street from Grant all the way to Hillside Avenue.[553] Twitchell was still alive at that time and probably could have had the artery maintained as Twitchell Street had he cared to, but he was apparently more concerned with memorializing others than with preserving his own legacy. He may have believed promoting his own historical significance was beneath his dignity, and was perhaps relying on his friends and colleagues to pay him a fitting tribute and secure his place in history. Whatever the case, Twitchell never said a word as his name faded from the map.

After Twitchell's death, the city of Santa Fe chose not to reinstate the name along the east end of Marcy Street, or to designate a different roadway with his name. The city's unwillingness to act is a mystery, especially since there was plenty of support for the idea within the community. In fact, the notion that Santa Fe should honor Twitchell by naming a street after him or building a monument to him was still being advanced by residents as late as 1952. The city never undertook any measures to memorialize him, however, so today no street in Santa Fe bears his name. This is ironic, considering Twitchell first suggested naming streets in the heart of the city after historical figures.[554]

That was not his only suggestion regarding the commemoration of New Mexico's pioneers either. One of his great passions had been placing historical markers in and around Santa Fe.[555] He had of course been behind the construction of the Cross of the Martyrs, but he was also responsible for getting the city to name the bridge at the north end of Grant avenue "El Puente de los Hidalgos," in honor of the Spaniards who colonized the area hundreds of years earlier.[556] Among his more notable accomplishments in regard to monumentalizing the state's past was the placement of markers along the Santa Fe Trail. Preserving the memories of bygone eras was no mere hobby for Twitchell; he was committed to maintaining the connection between New Mexico's past and present, and to making information about past exploits readily available to the state's young people. He believed "in the sentiment of these things and that this sentiment should be preserved."[557]

Twitchell had been adept at arousing appreciation for historic landmarks, for preserving them, and for "erecting memorials to famous figures in New Mexico's history."[558] His extensive political connections made him particularly effective in that regard. He seldom had to worry about a lack of support when he wanted to venerate someone he admired; or if he just wanted to play a practical joke, for that matter.

If a somewhat dubious tale is to be believed, then the all but forgotten ghost town of Waldo, New Mexico, was given its name by Ralph Twitchell. This now defunct burg (which amounted to a single cement foundation and a sign in 2005) came into being in the last decade of the nineteenth century when more than a dozen coke ovens were constructed along the railroad tracks to process coal from the mines at nearby Madrid for use by the Santa Fe Railroad. Legend has it that Twitchell, along with his friend and mentor, Henry Waldo, were once traveling past the little whistle-stop aboard a train, when the overwhelming reek of cow manure assaulted them. Seeking the source of the foul odor Waldo peered out the window only to be confronted by the name of his protégé and current traveling companion, emblazoned on a sign overhanging a series of crowded stock pens. Drawing Twitchell's attention to the sign that bore his name Waldo "teased his friend, saying 'I can't think of a more appropriate name for a bull-shipping point.'

But Twitchell had the last laugh; he used his political influence to change the name to Waldo."[559]

Without Ralph Twitchell's industry and advocacy, however, the historical preservation movement in Santa Fe was severely diminished. In the weeks and months following his funeral nothing appears to have been done to ensure the creation of a Twitchell monument, and as a result there was hardly a token of appreciation constructed within Santa Fe.

No monuments dedicated to the memory of R. E. Twitchell were erected outside of Santa Fe either, for that matter. In the years after his death, a majority of New Mexicans seem to have been all too willing to let Twitchell recede into the past without mention.

Eventually, the idea of erecting a proper monument to Ralph Twitchell was revisited by the State of New Mexico. A half-century after his death an initiative to commemorate Twitchell's contribution to the state emerged. In 1975, the New Mexico State Cultural Properties Review Committee included his name on a list of candidates submitted to Governor Jerry Apodaca, for consideration as the name of a new state building under construction at that time.[560] In the end, Twitchell was evidently not selected as the honoree, because no state building in Santa Fe bears his name.

By 1980 Ralph Twitchell appeared destined to become a footnote in New Mexico history. He was all but forgotten except among historians and scholars, who still recognized his books as seminal contributions to the historiography of the Southwest. Among those conscious of Twitchell's significance, as an author if nothing else, were members of the New Mexico Historical Society. Keen on preserving Twitchell's public memory, they moved to commemorate his contributions as a historian. Some six decades after his passing Twitchell was honored by the New Mexico Historical Society with a most fitting tribute. During the 1980s, the society created the Ralph Emerson Twitchell Award, honoring notable contributions in the arena of history, and added the accolade to their annual awards program.[561] The organization has continued to bestow this distinction upon scholars for over thirty years.

Still and all, the lack of a public monument commemorating R. E. Twitchell's myriad contributions to Santa Fe, New Mexico, and the country at large smacks of egregious oversight. The absence of a dedicatory marker within Santa Fe is particularly poignant, considering that the modern orientation of the city, with

144

its focus on historical tourism, is actually the embodiment of Twitchell's vision for his beloved city different. Santa Fe actually became the attraction Twitchell imagined and engendered roughly a century ago. As such, the city serves as a perfect testament to how much he helped shape modern New Mexico. While a monument or plaque bearing witness to his many noteworthy deeds would certainly be appropriate, it is perhaps unneeded, because contemporary Santa Fe is the Ralph Twitchell Monument. No etched stele, regardless of its message, could convey a more appropriate tribute.

Sources and Bibliography

Special Collections

Ralph Emerson Twitchell Collection. New Mexico State Library,
Records Center and Archives: Santa Fe, New Mexico.
Ralph Emerson Twitchell Papers 1896–1986. Fray Angelico Chavez
History Library and Photo Archives: Santa Fe, New Mexico.
Santa Fe County District Court Records. New Mexico State Library,
Records Center and Archives: Santa Fe, New Mexico.
Territorial Archive of New Mexico. New Mexico State Library, Records
Center and Archives: Santa Fe, New Mexico.

Legislative Acts

"An Act Relating to the Qualifications of All Public Officers of the
Territory of New Mexico, and Every County Thereof," C. B. 11, Chapter
1, Section 1: Approved January 4, 1893.

Newspapers

The Albuquerque Journal
The Albuquerque Morning Journal
The Albuquerque Tribune
The Arizona Republican
The Deming Headlight
The Farmington Enterprise
The Farmington Times-Hustler
The Galveston Daily News
The Indianapolis Sun

The Iola Daily Register
The Joplin Globe
The Las Vegas Daily Optic
The Lawrence Daily Journal-World
The Lawrence Journal World
The Los Angeles Times
The Oakland Tribune
The Reno Evening Gazette
The Rio Rancho Observer
The Rio Grande Republic
The Rio Grande Republican
The Roswell Daily Record
The Salt Lake Tribune
The San Antonio Light
The Santa Fe Daily Herald
The Santa Fe Daily New Mexican
The Santa Fe Daily Sun
The Santa Fe Herald
The Santa Fe New Mexican
The Santa Fe New Mexican Review
The Santa Fe New Mexican Review and Live Stock
The Santa Fe Sun
The Santa Fe Weekly Sun
The Santa Fe Weekly New Mexican Review
The Syracuse Herald
The Taos News
The Washington Post

Books

Anderson, George D. History of New Mexico: Its Resources and People vol. 1. Oakland: Pacific States Publishing Co., 1907.

Ball, Larry D. The United States Marshals of New Mexico and Arizona Territories 1846–1912. Albuquerque: University of New Mexico Press, 1978.

Bankcroft, Hubert Howe, and Henry Ebbeus Oak. History of Arizona and New Mexico: 1530–1888. Cambridge: Harvard University

Press, 1889.

Beck, Warren A. New Mexico: A History of Four Centuries. Norman: University of Oklahoma Press, 1963.

Bokovoy, Matthew F. The San Diego World's Fairs and Southwestern Memory 1880–1940. Albuquerque: University of New Mexico Press, 2005.

Caffey, David L. Frank Springer and New Mexico: From the Colfax County War to the Emergence of Modern Santa Fe. College Station: Texas A&M University Press, 2006.

Chavez, Thomas E. New Mexico Past and Future. Albuquerque: University of New Mexico Press, 2006.

Clark, Ira G. Water In New Mexico: A History of its Management and Use. Albuquerque: University of New Mexico Press, 1987.

Coan, Charles F. A History of New Mexico. Santa Fe: New Mexico Historical Society, 1925.

Etulian, Richard W. New Mexican Lives: Profiles and Historical Stories. Albuquerque: University of New Mexico Press, 2002.

Jenkins, Myra Ellen. A Brief History of New Mexico. Albuquerque: University of New Mexico Press, 1975.

Kenner, Charles L. A History of New Mexican-Plains Indian Relations. Norman: University of Oklahoma Press, 1969.

La Farge, Oliver. Santa Fe: The Autobiography of a Southwestern Town. Norman: University of Oklahoma Press, 1981.

Lamar, Howard R. The Far Southwest 1846–1912: A Territorial History. Albuquerque: University of New Mexico Press, 2000.

Larson, Robert W. New Mexico's Quest For Statehood 1846–1912. Albuquerque: University of New Mexico Press, 1968.

Marquez, Ruben Salaz. New Mexico: A Brief History. Albuquerque: Cosmic House, 2005.

Melzer, Richard. New Mexico: A Celebration of the Land of Enchantment. Layton: Gibbs Smith, 2011.

Otero, Miguel Antonio. My Life on the Frontier 1882–1897. Santa Fe: Sunstone Press, 2007.

Otero, Miguel Antonio. My Nine Years as Governor of the Territory of New Mexico 1897–1906. Santa Fe: Sunstone Press, 2007.

Prince, L. Bradford. A Concise History of New Mexico. Cedar Rapids: The Torch Press, 1914.

Read, Benjamin M. Illustrated History of New Mexico. Santa Fe: New Mexican Printing Co., 1912.

Romero, Orlando, Chair, Call for Papers Committee, Santa Fe 400th Commemorative Committee. All Trails Lead to Santa Fe, An

Anthology Commemorating the 400th Anniversary of the Founding of Santa Fe, New Mexico in 1610. Santa Fe: Sunstone Press, 2010.

Thomas, Benjamin M. Acts of the Legislative Assembly of the Territory of New Mexico Twenty-Ninth Session. Santa Fe: New Mexico Printing Company, 1891.

Tice, Henry Allen. Early Railroad Days in New Mexico. Santa Fe: Stagecoach Press, 1965.

Tobias, Henry J., and Charles E. Woodhouse. Santa Fe: A Modern History. Albuquerque: University of New Mexico Press, 2001.

Twitchell, Ralph Emerson. The Bench and Bar of New Mexico During the American Occupation: 1846–1850. Santa Fe: New Mexico Publishing Co., 1891.

Twitchell, Ralph Emerson. Genealogy of the Twitchell Family: Record of the Descendents of the Puritan Benjamin Twitchell. Rutland: The Tuttle Company Publishers, 1929.

Twitchell, Ralph Emerson. The History of the Military Occupation of the Territory of New Mexico from 1846 to 1851 by the Government of the United States. Danville: Interstate Printers and Publishers, 1909. New Edition, Santa Fe: Sunstone Press, 2007, with title, The Military Occupation of the Territory of New Mexico from 1846 to 1851.

Twitchell, Ralph Emerson. The Leading Facts of New Mexico History: Volumes 1-5. Cedar Rapids: The Torch Press, 1911–1917. New Edition, Santa Fe: Sunstone Press, 2007.

Twitchell, Ralph Emerson. The Spanish Archives of New Mexico. Santa Fe: Sunstone Press, 2008.

Twitchell, Ralph Emerson. Old Santa Fe. Santa Fe: Sunstone Press, 2007.

Weigle, Marta. Telling New Mexico: A New History. Santa Fe: Museum of New Mexico Press, 2009.

West, Elizabeth. Santa Fe: 400 Years, 400 Questions. Santa Fe: Sunstone Press, 2012.

Westphall, Victor. Thomas Benton Catron and His Era. Tucson: University of Arizona Press, 1973.

Wilson, Chris. The Myth of Santa Fe: Creating a Modern Regional Tradition. Albuquerque: University of New Mexico Press, 1997.

Historical Journals

Bloom Lansing B. and Paul A. F. Walter. "Ralph Emerson Twitchell." The New Mexico Historical Review, vol. 1. (1926): 78-85.

Dargan, Marion. "New Mexico's Fight for Statehood 1895–1912," The New Mexico Historical Review, vol. 14, no. 1. (1939): 1-33.

Dargan, Marion. "New Mexico's Fight for Statehood 1895–1912," The New Mexico Historical Review, vol. 14, no. 2. (1939): 121-125.

"Estelle Bennett Twitchell." El Palacio, vol. 59, no. 11. (1952): 361-362.

"Helping Win The War." El Palacio, vol. 5, no. 2. (1918): 24.

"HSNM Solicits Award Nominations." La Cronica de Nuevo Mexico, issue 23. (1986): 4.

Jenkins, Myra Ellen. "A Dedication to the Memory of Ralph Emerson Twitchell 1859–1925." Arizona and the West: A Quarterly Journal of History, vol. 8. (1966): 103-106.

Padilla, Camilo. "Coronel Ralph Emerson Twitchell.- Historiador, Autor, Orador y Defensor del Bien Comun." Revista Ilustrada, vol. 9. (1916): 8-10, translation 1-8.

"Ralph Emerson Twitchell." El Palacio, vol. 19, no. 1. (1925): 83-87.

Twitchell, Ralph E. "Stage Driver to Railroad President." The Santa Fe Magazine, vol. 17, no. 2. (1923): 49-51.

Walter, Paul A. F. "Important Appointment." El Palacio, vol. 10, no. 12. (1921): 11.

Walter, Paul A. F. "Colonel Ralph E. Twitchell." El Palacio, vol. 11, no. 4. (1921): 59-60.

Websites (active as of the date of publication)

Conservation Conferences. www.theodore-roosevelt.com.

CRW Flags Inc. www.crwflags.com.

New Mexico Office of the State Historian. www.newmexicohistory.org.

Sanborn Map Company. www.sanborn.umi.com.

San Diego History Center. www.sandiegohistory.org.

The American Presidency Project. www.presidency.ucsb.edu.

Water and Wastes Digest. www.wwdmag.com/new-mexico-farmers-bring-about-deal-relinquish-reservoir-water-texas.

NOTES

1. Bench and Bar of New Mexico During the American Occupation 1846–1850 was commissioned by the New Mexico Bar Association; History of the Military Occupation of the Territory of New Mexico from 1816 to 1851 by the Government of the United States (Danville, Illinios: Interstate Printers and Publishers, 1909); The Leading Facts of New Mexico History: Volumes 1-5 (Cedar Rapids, Iowa: The Torch Press, 1911–1917); The Spanish Archives of New Mexico (New Mexico: The Torch Press, 1914); Spanish Colonization in New Mexico in the Onate and De Vargas Periods (Historical Society of New Mexico, 1919); Dr. Josiah Gregg: Historian of the Santa Fe Trail (Santa Fe, New Mexico: Santa Fe New Mexican Publishing Corp., 1924); Old Santa Fe (Santa Fe, New Mexico: Santa Fe New Mexican Publishing Corp., 1925); Genealogy of the Twitchell Family (Rutland, Vermont: The Tuttle Company Publishers, 1929).

2. New Mexico State Records Center and Archives: 1205 Camino Carlos Rey, Santa Fe, New Mexico.

3. Arizona and the West: A Quarterly Journal of History Vol. 8 (Tucson, Arizona: 1966); The New Mexico Historical Review Vol. 1 (Published Quarterly by The Historical Society of New Mexico at the Museum Press Santa Fe, New Mexico: 1926); El Palacio; The Santa Fe Magazine.

4. Ralph Emerson Twitchell Papers 1896–1986, Museum of New Mexico, Palace of the Governors, Fray Angelico Chavez History Library: P.O. BOX 2087 Santa Fe, New Mexico.

5. Marta Weigle, Telling New Mexico: A New History (Santa Fe, New Mexico: Museum of New Mexico Press, 2009); Ruben Salaz Marquez, New Mexico: A Brief Multi-History (Albuquerque, New Mexico: Cosmic House, 2005); Benjamin M. Read, Illustrated History of New Mexico (New Mexican Printing Co., 1912); History of New Mexico: Its Resources and People Vol. 1 (Los Angeles, California: Pacific States Publishing Co., 1907); J. Michael Pattison, "Four Gentlemen Historians of New Mexico" (Master thesis, New Mexico Highlands University, 1992).

6. Hubert Howe Bankcroft and Henry Ebbeus Oak, History of Arizona and New Mexico 1530–1888 (History Company, Harvard University, 1889); Warren A. Beck, New Mexico: A History of Four Centuries: (Standard Survey, 1962); Thomas E. Chavez, New Mexico Past and Future (Albuquerque, New Mexico: University of New Mexico Press,

Oct. 1, 2006); Charles F. Coan, A History of New Mexico (Santa Fe, New Mexico: New Mexico Historical Society, 1925); Myra Ellen Jenkins, A Brief History of New Mexico (Albuquerque, New Mexico: University of New Mexico Press, 1st edition Jan. 1, 1975); L. Bradford Prince, A Concise History of New Mexico (Cedar Rapids, Iowa: The Torch Press, 2nd edition, 1914); Frank Driver Reeve, History of New Mexico (Lewis Historical Publishing Co., 1st edition, 1961); Don Bullis, New Mexico: A Biographical Dictionary 1540–1980 (Rio Grande Books, Oct. 13, 2006); Richard W. Etulian, New Mexican Lives: Profiles and Historical Stories (Albuquerque, New Mexico: University of New Mexico Press, Feb. 1, 2002); George Peter Hammond, The Story of New Mexico: Its History and Government (Albuquerque, New Mexico: University of New Mexico Press, 1945); Charles L. Kenner, A History of New Mexican-Plains Indian Relations (University of Oklahoma Press, 1969); Oliver La Farge, Santa Fe: The Autobiography of a Southwestern Town (University of Oklahoma Press, March, 1981); Marc Simmons, Yesterday in Santa Fe: Episodes in a Turbulent History (San Marcos Press, 1st edition, 1969); Henry Allen Tice, Early Railroad Days in New Mexico (Santa Fe, New Mexico: Stagecoach Press, 1965); Henry J. Tobias, Charles E. Woodhouse, Santa Fe: A Modern History (Albuquerque, New Mexico: University of New Mexico Press, 2001); Howard R. Lamar, The Far Southwest 1846–1912: A Territorial History (Albuquerque, New Mexico: University of New Mexico Press, revised edition, Sept. 1, 2000).

7. Victor Westphall, Thomas Benton Catron and His Era (Tucson, Arizona: University of Arizona Press, 1973); David L. Caffey, Frank Springer and New Mexico: From the Colfax County War to the Emergence of Modern Santa Fe (College Station, Texas: Texas A&M University Press, 2006); Miguel Antonio Otero, My Nine Years as Governor of the Territory of New Mexico 1897–1906 (Santa Fe, New Mexico: Sunstone Press, 2007); David L. Caffey, Chasing the Santa Fe Ring: Power and Privilege in Territorial New Mexico (Albuquerque, New Mexico: University of New Mexico Press, 2014); David V. Holtby, Forty-Seventh Star: New Mexico's Struggle for Statehood (Norman, Oklahoma: University of Oklahoma Press, 2012).

8. Richard N. Ellis, New Mexico, Past and Present (Albuquerque, New Mexico: University of New Mexico Press, 1971).

9. Quote from the title page of R. E. Twitchell, The Leading Facts of New Mexico History, vol. 2.

10. Ralph Emerson Twitchell, Genealogy of the Twitchell Family: Record of the Descendents of the Puritan Benjamin Twitchell (Vermont: Tuttle Company Publishers, 1929), xii.

11. Benjamin Twitchell crossed the Atlantic in 1630, while still an adolescent: see Ralph Emerson Twitchell, Genealogy of the Twitchell Family: Record of the Descendents of the Puritan Benjamin Twitchell (Vermont: Tuttle Company Publishers, 1929), xvii-xvx.

12. Ibid., xii.

13. Ibid., xii.

14. Ibid., xi.

15. Ibid., xxii.

16. Ibid., 308.

17. Ibid., 67.

18. Ibid., 88.

19. Ibid., xxxiii.

20. Ibid., 153.

21a. Ibid., 273.

21b. Ibid., 273-274

21c. Ibid., 446.

22. Ibid., 448.

23. Ibid., 444.

24. "Restore the Old Veranda," The Santa Fe New Mexican, March 7, 1905, 1.

25. Twitchell, Genealogy, 274.

26. Ibid., 273.

27. Ibid., 444.

28. "Down The Old Santa Fe Trail: 50 Years Ago: From the Files of The New Mexican, February 20, 1924," The Santa Fe New Mexican, February 20, 1974, 4.

29. Twitchell, Genealogy, 444.

30. Iola Daily Register, February 22, 1923, 4.

31. Using a specious telegram delivered by someone in the guise of a Western Union employee, Twitchell and his accomplices convinced the Chancellor of the University that one of the Regents had died. The phony communiqué was so believable that memorial services were held at the university chapel for the supposedly deceased individual before the practical joke was uncovered. Twitchell and the other tricksters then gathered for a mock mourning parade to gloat over the success of their stunt. The administration failed to see the humor, however, and swiftly punished the perpetrators: see "Recalls Big Hoax," Lawrence Daily Journal-World, August 29, 1925, 1.

32. Ibid., 1.

33. Myra Ellen Jenkins, "A Dedication to the Memory of Ralph Emerson Twitchell 1859-1925," Arizona and the West 8 (1966): 103.

34. Santa Fe Daily New Mexican, September 19, 1894, 1.

35. Gussie Fauntleroy, "Ralph Emerson Twitchell Took on Large Orders," The Santa Fe New Mexican, August 16, 1999, F3.

36. Howard R. Lamar, The Far Southwest 1846-1912: A Territorial History Revised Edition (Albuquerque: University of New Mexico Press, 1966): 154.

37. Jenkins, "Ralph Emerson Twitchell," 103.

38. Twitchell, Genealogy, 305.

39. Fauntleroy, "Ralph Emerson Twitchell Took on Large Orders," F3.

40. Marion Dargan, "New Mexico's Fight for Statehood 1895-1912," The New Mexico Historical Review vol.xiv (The Historical Society of New Mexico, January 1939, no. 1): 5.

41. Oath of Commissioned Officer NM Militia: May 12, 1884 (New Mexico State Record Center and Archives, Territorial Archive of New Mexico) Microfilm collection, Roll 86, Frames 904,905.

42. Fauntleroy, "Ralph Emerson Twitchell Took on Large Orders," F3.

43. Ibid., F3.

44. Las Vegas Daily Optic, August 10, 1886, 4.

45. Twitchell, Genealogy, 445.

46. Santa Fe New Mexican Review, January 8, 1885, 4.

47. Santa Fe Weekly New Mexican Review and Live Stock, June 10, 1886, 3.

48. Twitchell, Genealogy, 444.

49. Camilo Padilla, "Coronel Ralph E. Twitchell.- Historiador, Autor, Orador y Defensor del Bien Comun.," Revista Ilustrada, June, 1916, vol. IX, 1.

50. Santa Fe Daily New Mexican, November 28, 1885, 4.

51. The Santa Fe Weekly Sun, August 8, 1891, 4.

52. Las Vegas Daily Optic, August 10, 1886, 4.

53. Santa Fe Daily New Mexican, November 5, 1887, 4.

54. Twitchell, Genealogy, 575.

55. Padilla, "Coronel Ralph E. Twitchell," 2.

56. The Santa Fe Weekly Sun, August 29, 1891, 4.

57. The Santa Fe Weekly Sun, November 14, 1891, 4.

58. Las Vegas Daily Optic, June 4, 1895, 3.

59. Twitchell, Genealogy, 575.

60. Ibid., 575.

61. "Estelle Bennett Twitchell," El Palacio vol. 59, no. 11 (November 1952): 361.

62. Ralph Emerson Twitchell, The Leading Facts of New Mexico History, vol. 5 (Iowa: Torch Press, 1917), 158-159.

63. Twitchell, Genealogy, 446.

64. "Colonel Ralph E. Twitchell Dies In Los Angeles and State Mourns Brilliant Barrister, Historian," The Santa Fe New Mexican, August 26, 1925, 1.

65. Marc Simmons, "The Story Behind N.M. History Author," The Santa Fe New Mexican, August 30, 2008.

66. "Estelle Bennett Twitchell," 361.

67. Twitchell, The Leading Facts of New Mexico History, vol. 5, 158.

68. Lansing B. Bloom and Paul A. F. Walter, editors, "Ralph Emerson Twitchell" The New Mexico Historical Review, vol. 1 (Santa Fe, The Museum Press, 1926), 78.

69. David L. Caffey, Frank Springer and New Mexico: From the Colfax County War to the Emergence of Modern Santa Fe (College Station: Texas A&M University Press, 2006), 112.

70. "Ralph Emerson Twitchell," El Palacio vol. 19, no. 1 (September 1, 1925): 85.

71. The Santa Fe New Mexican, June 17, 1883, 4.

72. "Colonel Ralph E. Twitchell Dies In Los Angeles and State Mourns Brilliant Barrister, Historian," 1.

73. Bloom and Walter, "Ralph Emerson Twitchell," 78.

74. "Colonel Twitchell Pays Tribute To Late Judge Waldo," The Santa Fe New Mexican, September 19, 1919, 7.

75. "Personal Mention," Lawrence Journal World, October 18, 1898, 4.

76. History of New Mexico: Its Resources and People, vol. 1 (Pacific States Publishing Co. 1907), 300.

77. Letter from Ralph Twitchell to Theodore Roosevelt, Ralph E. Twitchell papers, New Mexico State Record Center and Archives.

78. Bloom and Walter, "Ralph Emerson Twitchell," 78.

79. "The New Receiver," The Santa Fe New Mexican, September 17, 1917, 4.

80. "Holloman Removes R. C. Ely," The Santa Fe New Mexican, September 15, 1917, 1.

81. Twitchell, Genealogy, 446.

82. "Court Compliments Receiver Twitchell," newspaper clipping from the Ralph Emerson Twitchell Papers, box 8, folder 10, Fray Angelico Chavez History Library and Photo Archives.

83. "Can You Pick The New Federal Judge? Twitchell And Holloman, Latest," The Santa Fe New Mexican, July 27, 1922, 2.

84. "R. E. Twitchell Wouldn't Take U. S. Judgeship," The Santa Fe New Mexican, July 28, 1922, 5.

85. Rio Grande Republican, September 9, 1892, 1.

86. "Attorneys vs. Office Holders," Santa Fe Daily Herald, September 10, 1888, 4.

87. "L. (Lebaron) Bradford Prince," http://www.newmexicohistory.org/people/l-lebaron-bradford-prince.

88. "Letter to L. Bradford Prince from R. E. Twitchell, April 2, 1889" (New Mexico State Records Center and Archives), Territorial Archives of New Mexico, Microfilms, roll 103, frame 67.

89. The Santa Fe Herald, November 26, 1888, 2.

90. Twitchell, Genealogy, 444.

91. "The Territory of New Mexico, ex rel. Jacob H. Crist v. Ralph E. Twitchell," Santa Fe County District Court Records: Civil #2626. Box 40, 1888–1889, New Mexico State Records Center and Archives.

92. "The Territory of New Mexico, ex rel. Jacob H. Crist v. Ralph E. Twitchell," Santa Fe County District Court Records: Civil #2626. Box 40, 1888–1889, New Mexico State Records Center and Archives.

93. Ibid.

94. Ibid.

95. Ibid.

96a. Ibid.

96b. Collection Guide, Collection of New Mexican Mining Documents 1881-1901 MS237, Special Collections, University of Arizona. http://speccoll.library.arizona.edu/collections/collection-new-mexican-mining-documents.

97. The Santa Fe Sun printed its first issue on January 4, 1890, less than eight months after Crist lost his court case against Twitchell, and remained in circulation until June 1893, one month after Twitchell vacated the DA's office.

98. "Political Persecution" Santa Fe Sun, July 26, 1890, 4.

99. Miguel Antonio Otero, My Life on the Frontier, 1882–1897 (Santa Fe: Sunstone Press, 2007), 266-268.

100. Larry D. Ball, The United States Marshals of New Mexico and Arizona Territories 1846–1912 (Albuquerque: University of New Mexico Press, 1978), 151.

101. "A Political Court," Santa Fe Sun, August 30, 1890, 1.

102. "Rumors Refuted," Santa Fe Sun, June 7, 1890, 4.

103. "Saturday Salad," Santa Fe Sun, August 16, 1890, 1.

104. Santa Fe Sun, August 26,1890, 2.

105. Santa Fe Sun, August 23, 1890, 1.

106. "A Political Court," Santa Fe Sun, August 30, 1890, 1.

107. "For The Council—Ralph Emerson Twitchell," Santa Fe Sun, May 10, 1890, 2.

108. "A Political Court," Santa Fe Sun, August 30, 1890, 1.

109. "Situation In The Northwest, The Convention, General Politics, and The Court Terms," Santa Fe Sun, September 20, 1890, 1.

110. Santa Fe Sun, September 20, 1890, 2.

111. Ibid., 2.

112. Santa Fe Sun, October 25, 1890, 4.

113. Benjamin M. Thomas, "Acts of the Legislative Assembly of the Territory of New Mexico 29th Session" Prepared for publication by Benjamin M. Thomas, Secretary of the Territory, (Santa Fe: New Mexico Printing Company, 1891).

114. Santa Fe Sun, December 27, 1890, 4.

115. "District Attorney R. E. Twitchell," Santa Fe Daily New Mexican, January 26, 1891, 6.

116. "District Court," Santa Fe Daily New Mexican, February 9, 1891, 5.

117. "The Jury Law Unconstitutional," Santa Fe Daily Sun, February 15, 1891, 4.

118. Ibid., 4.

119. New Mexico State Records Center and Archives, Santa Fe County District Court, Criminal: R. Martinez et al., Murder, Box 59, Folder 2509, (1890).

120. "Judge Seeds' Decision In The Faustin Ortiz Indictments," Santa Fe Daily New Mexican, February 16, 1891, 3.

121. Ibid., 3.

122. Santa Fe Daily Sun, February 15, 1891, 2.

123. Santa Fe Daily Sun, February 18, 1891, 2.

124. Ball, United States Marshals of New Mexico and Arizona, 152.

125. "Hon. R. E. Twitchell," Santa Fe Daily New Mexican, September 19, 1891, 1.

126. Otero, My Life on the Frontier, 266.

127. Ball, United States Marshals of New Mexico and Arizona, 153.

128. Ibid., 153.

129. "Letter from Governor Thornton to Ralph E. Twitchell, May 26, 1893" (New Mexico State Records Center and Archives), Territorial Archives of New Mexico, Microfilms, roll 125, frames 743-746.

130. "100 Years Ago: From The New Mexican, August 24, 1890," The Santa Fe New Mexican, August 24, 1990, B-2.

131. The act that Twitchell was charged with being in violation of made persons who were holders or receivers of the territory's public moneys ineligible to hold public office. There is no proof that Twitchell was ever in breach of the act: see "An Act Relating to the Qualifications of All Public Officers of the Territory of New Mexico, and Every County Thereof. C. B. 11; Approved January 4, 1893. Section 1, Chapter 1."

132. "Letter from Governor Thornton to R. E. Twitchell, May 26, 1893," (New Mexico State Records Center and Archives), Territorial Archives of New Mexico, Microfilms, roll 125, frames 494, 746.

133. Rio Grande Republican, September 9, 1892, 1.

134. "Colonel Twitchell," Rio Grande Republican, April 22, 1910, 1.

135. "Hon. R. E. Twitchell," Santa Fe Daily New Mexican, September 19, 1891, 1.

136. "Twitchell For Mayor," Santa Fe Weekly New Mexican Review, March 30, 1893, 3.

137. Ibid., 3.

138. "The Winners Named," Santa Fe Weekly New Mexican Review, March 30, 1893, 4.

139. Twitchell, Genealogy, 445.

140. Henry J. Tobias and Charles E. Woodhouse, Santa Fe: A Modern History 1880–1999 (Albuquerque: University of New Mexico Press, 2001), 41.

141. Ibid., 30.

142. Santa Fe Weekly New Mexican Review, March 30, 1893, 4.

143a. "The City Council," Santa Fe Weekly New Mexican Review, April 20, 1893, 4.

143b. Ibid., 4.

144a. Tobias and Woodhouse, Santa Fe, 41.

144b. Ibid., 41-43.

145. Ibid., 41.

146a. Ibid., 41.

146b. Ibid., 41.

147. Ibid., 43.

148a. Fauntleroy, "Ralph Emerson Twitchell Took on Large Orders," F3.

148b. Ibid., F3.

149. Marion Dargan, "New Mexico's Fight for Statehood 1895–1912," The New Mexico Historical Review 14, no. 2 (1939): 123.

150. Tobias and Woodhouse, Santa Fe, 43.

151. Mayor Twitchell was even involved in a shootout while helping law enforcement personnel serve an arrest warrant: see "A Midnight Brawl," Santa Fe Weekly New Mexican Review, April 5, 1894, 7.

152. Padilla, "Coronel Ralph E. Twitchell," 3.

153. "Colonel Twitchell," Rio Grande Republican, April 22, 1910, 1.

154. "Can't Boost Unless There's A Change In City Methods, Says Twitchell," The Santa Fe New Mexican, February 22, 1915, 4.

155. "Campaign Crumbs," Santa Fe New Mexican Review, October 22, 1884, 4.

156. "Hon. R. E. Twitchell," Santa Fe Daily New Mexican, September 19, 1891, 1.

157. Ibid., 1.

158. Las Vegas Daily Optic, March 2, 1892, 4.

159. "Republican Club Organized," Roswell Daily Record, October 12, 1916, 4.

160. "Hon. R. E. Twitchell," Santa Fe Daily New Mexican, September 19, 1891, 1.

161a. "Political Budget," Santa Fe Weekly New Mexican Review, March 9, 1893, 4.

161b. Ibid., 4.

161c. Ibid., 4.

162. Bloom and Walter, "Ralph Emerson Twitchell," 79.

163. Padilla, "Coronel Ralph E. Twitchell," 3.

164. Ibid., 3.

165. Ibid., 3.

166. Victor Westphall, Thomas Benton Catron and His Era (Tucson: University of Arizona Press, 1973), 261.

167. Ibid., 261.

168. Ibid., 261, 262, 390.

169. "Statehood and Andrews Slogan of Big Republican Rally," The Santa Fe New Mexican, October 31, 1908, 6.

170. Charles F. Coan, A History of New Mexico, vol. 1 (New York: The American Historical Society Inc., 1925), 411.

171. Ibid., 7.

172a. "Plenty of Congressional Timber," Las Vegas Daily Optic, June 27, 1890, 1.

172b. Ibid., 1.

173. Albuquerque Evening Citizen, April 25, 1901, quoted in Robert W. Larson, New Mexico's Quest for Statehood, 1846–1912 (Albuquerque: University of New Mexico Press, 1968), 200.

174. Marion Dargan, "New Mexico's Fight for Statehood 1895–1912: II. The Attitude of the Territorial Press," New Mexico Historical Review vol. 14, no. 2 (The Historical Society of New Mexico, 1939), 121.

175. Marion Dargan, "New Mexico's Fight for Statehood 1895–1912: I. The Political Leaders of the Latter Half of the 1890's and Statehood," New Mexico Historical Review vol. 14, no. 1 (The Historical Society of New Mexico, 1939), 9-10.

176. Ibid., 6.

177. "Andrews and the Irrigation Congress," Farmington Enterprise, June 26, 1908, 4.

178. Mark B. Thompson, "Rodey, Bernard and the Jointure Movement in the U.S. Congress," New Mexico Office of the State Historian, www.newmexicohistory.org/filedetails_docs.php?fileID=23337.

179. "Andrews and the Irrigation Congress," Farmington Enterprise, June 26, 1908, 4.

180. Ibid., 4.

181a. "Statehood and Andrews Slogan of Big Republican Rally," The Santa Fe New Mexican, October 31, 1908, 6.

181b. Ibid., 6.

181c. Ibid., 6.

181d. Ibid., 6.

181e. "Statehood and Andrews Slogan of Big Republican Rally," The Santa Fe New Mexican, October 31, 1908, 1, 6, 7.

182. "Women Register Firm Protest on New State Flag," The Santa Fe New Mexican, March 17, 1915, 5.

183. Howard Bryan, "Off the Beaten Path," Albuquerque Tribune, May 9, 1963, C-4.

184a. New Mexico (U.S.) – CRW Flags Inc. www.crwflags.com/fotw/flags/us-nm.html#his.

184b. Ibid.

185. "Colonel Twitchell Wont Run, Says," The Santa Fe New Mexican, July 31, 1914, 1.
186. "Helping Win The War," El Palacio vol. 5, no. 2 (1918): 24.
187a. Jenkins, "Ralph Emerson Twitchell," 104.
187b. Ibid., 104.
188. "In Old Mexico," The Santa Fe New Mexican, September 23, 1899, 4.
189. Miguel Otero, My Nine Years as Governor of the Territory of New Mexico 1897–1906 (Santa Fe: Sunstone Press, 2007), 42.
190. "In Old Mexico," The Santa Fe New Mexican, 4.
191. The Square Deal #2, August 30, 1919, issued by The Roosevelt Memorial Association, Ralph Emerson Twitchell Collection, (New Mexico State Records Center and Archives).
192. "Ralph E. Twitchell Heads Committee on Inauguration Plans," Albuquerque Morning Journal, November 16, 1920, 5.
193. "Twitchell Appointed Special Attorney," Deming Headlight, May 20, 1921, 5.
194. "Old Events Recalled," Albuquerque Journal, June 1, 1940, 10.
195. "Twitchell Appointed Special Attorney," Deming Headlight, May 20, 1921, 5.
196. Paul A. F. Walter, "Important Appointment," El Palacio vol. X, no. 12 (May 16, 1921): 11.
197. Ibid., 11.
198. Rick Romancito, "Nature and History of Land Conflicts," Taos News, July 26, 1990, B-4.
199. Ibid., B-4.
200. Paul A. F. Walter, "Colonel Ralph E. Twitchell," El Palacio vol. 11, no. 4 (August 15, 1921): 59.
201. Ibid., 59.
202. Romancito, "Nature and History of Land Conflicts," B-4.
203. Ibid., B-4.
204. "Bill Proposed to Give Relief to Buyers of Indian Lands," The Santa Fe New Mexican, July 22, 1922, 3.
205. "Washington Notes," Oakland Tribune, January 16, 1923, 11.
206. "Mrs. Atwood Brands All Indian Policy as Inhumane and Expensive," The Santa Fe New Mexican, January 22, 1923, 1, 3.
207. "Twitchell Says Charley Catron Really Wrote Much of Indian Bill," The Santa Fe New Mexican, August 7, 1922, 2.
208. Romancito, "Nature and History of Land Conflicts," B-4.
209. "Garfield Submits Report to Exonerate Ex-Indian Attorney and Takes Hot Shot at Fall," The Santa Fe New Mexican, February 10, 1923, 6.
210. "Mrs. Atwood Brands All Indian Policy as Inhumane and Expensive," 1,3.
211. "Garfield Submits Report to Exonerate Ex-Indian Attorney and Takes Hot Shot at Fall," 6.
212. "Mrs. Atwood Brands All Indian Policy as Inhumane and Expensive," 1,3.
213. "Walker Thinks Renehan as a Religious Exhorter Shows More Heat Than Light; Attorney Has a Very Merry Time With Lengthy Speech," The Santa Fe New Mexican, January 4, 1924, 2.
214. Ira G. Clark, Water In New Mexico: A History of its Management and Use (Albuquerque: University of New Mexico Press, 1987), 606, 607.
215. "Mrs. Atwood Brands All Indian Policy as Inhumane and Expensive," 1, 3.

216. "Garfield Submits Report to Exonerate Ex-Indian Attorney and Takes Hot Shot at Fall," 6.

217. Ibid., 6.

218. "Colonel Ralph E. Twitchell Dies In Los Angeles and State Mourns Brilliant Barrister, Historian," 4.

219. The Santa Fe New Mexican, February 13, 1917, 6.

220. "Colonel Ralph E. Twitchell Dies in Los Angeles and State Mourns Brilliant Barrister, Historian," 4.

221. Simmons, "The Story Behind N. M. History Author."

222. "Sauce for the Sociable," Santa Fe New Mexican Review, March 15, 1884, 4.

223. "The New Club," Santa Fe Daily New Mexican, March 13, 1891, 7.

224. "City Government," Santa Fe Weekly New Mexican Review, June 7, 1894, 1.

225. "City Council," Santa Fe Weekly New Mexican Review, July 26, 1894, 10.

226. "Fort Marcy…," The Santa Fe New Mexican, September 3, 1972, 4.

227. The American Presidency Project, Presidential Proclamations, Theodore Roosevelt. "Proclamation 514 – Grant of Fort Marcy Military Reservation to the Town of Santa Fe, New Mexico" www.presidency.ucsb.edu/proclamations.php?year=1904&Submit=DISPLAY.

228. Tobias and Woodhouse, Santa Fe, 51.

229. Ibid., 51.

230. Bloom and Walter, "Ralph Emerson Twitchell," 83.

231. "Ringing Appeal by Twitchell To People of New Mexico To Make the Capital Great," The Santa Fe New Mexican, February 13, 1917, 5.

232. Bloom and Walter, "Ralph Emerson Twitchell," 83.

233. Tobias and Woodhouse, Santa Fe, 51.

234. Bloom and Walter, "Ralph Emerson Twitchell," 82.

235. Jenkins, "Ralph Emerson Twitchell," 104.

236. Twitchell belonged to the New Mexico Archaeological Society, the Museum of New Mexico, and the School of American Research: see Bloom and Walter, "Ralph Emerson Twitchell," 82.

237. Tobias and Woodhouse, Santa Fe, 74-77.

238. Chris Wilson, The Myth of Santa Fe: Creating a Modern Regional Tradition (Albuquerque: University of New Mexico Press, 1997), 236.

239. Ibid., 236.

240. Ibid., 237.

241. Ibid., 124.

242. Ibid., 122.

243. Ibid., 122.

244. Bloom and Walter, "Ralph Emerson Twitchell," 81.

245. "Can't Boost Unless There's A Change In City Methods, Says Twitchell," 4.

246. "Corporal's Guard of Faithful Braves Roaring Deluge to Attend Meeting," The Santa Fe New Mexican, June 17, 1914, 3.

247. "Montrose, Colorado, Has Heard About Our Wants," The Santa Fe New Mexican, February 10, 1915, 8.

248. "Justice R. H. Hanna Elected President of Chamber of Commerce at Annual Meet," The Santa Fe New Mexican, April 28, 1916, 5.
249. Ibid., 5.
250. Ibid., 5.
251. "Mass Meeting Of Great Importance," The Santa Fe New Mexican, March 2, 1916, 2.
252. "Chamber of Commerce Elects Twitchell President; Enthusiastic Meeting Starts Big Program for Year," The Santa Fe New Mexican, April 7, 1920, 3.
253. "Chamber of Commerce Takes Hold Enthusiastically of Plan to Hold Annual De Vargas Pageant in Santa Fe," The Santa Fe New Mexican, August 2, 1916, 3.
254. The tradition sprang from a vow made by Don Diego De Vargas during the reconquest of Santa Fe, in which he swore that if he were victorious he would commemorate the day his forces re-entered the city with an annual parade and a vesper service: see "Fiesta resurged in '20s as a tourist attraction," The Santa Fe New Mexican, September 5, 1999, F8.
255. "De Vargas Pledge Kept Through Two And Half Centuries," The Santa Fe New Mexican, August 30, 1957, 9.
256. "Chamber of Commerce Takes Hold Enthusiastically of Plan to Hold Annual De Vargas Pageant in Santa Fe," The Santa Fe New Mexican, August 2, 1916, 3.
257. Ibid., 3.
258. Ibid., 3.
259. Ibid., 3.
260. Ibid., 3.
261. Ibid., 3.
262. "Santa Fe Wants Grand Fiesta to Be Permanent; Business Men at Museum Banquet Pledge $2,500," The Santa Fe New Mexican, October 29, 1919, 6.
263. "Colonel Twitchell," Santa Fe New Mexican, April 3, 1920, 4.
264a. "30 Blocks To Be Paved In Old Santa Fe," The Santa Fe New Mexican, June 20, 1919, 1.
264b. Ibid., 1.
265. Ibid., 1.
266. "Paving, Surfacing, Sewer, Drainage Program Formally Initiated by City Council in Resolutions Passed Last Night; Most Comprehensive Plan," The Santa Fe New Mexican, June 27, 1919, 5.
267. "Santa Fe to Put on Historic Pageant on September 12," The Santa Fe New Mexican, April 30, 1919, 6.
268. Ibid., 6.
269. Ibid., 6.
270. Ibid., 6.
271. "The Fiesta," The Santa Fe New Mexican, September 15, 1919, 4.
272. Ibid., 4.
273. Ibid., 4.
274. "Fiesta of Santa Fe in Autumn; To Show 1000 Years of History; Many Organizations Participate," The Santa Fe New Mexican, June 28, 1919, 5.
275. Ibid., 5.
276. "Preparing For Fiesta," The Santa Fe New Mexican, August 22, 1919, 8.

277. "Fiesta of Santa Fe in Autumn; To Show 1000 Years of History; Many Organizations Participate," 5.
278. Ibid., 5.
279. "Old Mail-Clad Conquistadores and Gen. Kearny to Come to Santa Fe; You Will See Weird Dances of Pueblos, and Picturesque Ones of Spain; Stage Coach Days of Blood and Thunder Again in Fiesta Next Week," The Santa Fe New Mexican, September 6, 1919, 5.
280. "Indians Gather From Near and Far in Santa Fe for Picturesque and Brilliant Tribal Ceremonials, Dances and Races at Fiesta," The Santa Fe New Mexican, September 11, 1919, 6.
281. "General Barnett and Party at Bishop's Lodge; Preparations for Fiesta Practically Complete," The Santa Fe New Mexican, September 10, 1919, 6.
282. Ibid., 6.
283. "Indians Gather From Near and Far in Santa Fe for Picturesque and Brilliant Tribal Ceremonials, Dances and Races at Fiesta," 6.
284. Ibid., 6.
285. Ibid., 6.
286. "De Vargas Will Enter Santa Fe in State and Take the City," The Santa Fe New Mexican, September 11, 1919, 6.
287. Ibid., 6.
288. Ibid., 6.
289. Ibid., 6.
290. "Official Program of Events of the Santa Fe Fiesta," The Santa Fe New Mexican, September 10, 1919, 1.
291. "General Kearny Occupies City; Another Impressive Spectacle of Santa Fe's History Reproduced," The Santa Fe New Mexican, September 13, 1919, 5.
292. "Final Indian Dances and Fiesta Scenes Staged in Museum When Storm Breaks," The Santa Fe New Mexican, September 15, 1919, 2.
293. "Santa Fe Wants Grand Fiesta to Be Permanent; Business Men at Museum Banquet Pledge $2,500," The Santa Fe New Mexican, October 29, 1919, 6.
294. Ibid., 6.
295. Ibid., 6.
296. Ibid., 6.
297. Ibid., 6.
298. "Fifty at Museum Night Supper; Community, Music, and Drama Chief Themes of Discussion," The Santa Fe New Mexican, November 8, 1919, 2.
299. "Colonel Twitchell," The Santa Fe New Mexican, April 3, 1920, 4.
300. "Chamber of Commerce Elects Twitchell President; Enthusiastic Meeting Starts Big Program for Year," The Santa Fe New Mexican, April 7, 1920, 3.
301. Ibid., 3.
302. Ibid., 3.
303. Ibid., 3.
304. Ibid., 3.
305. Ibid., 3.

306. "Commerce Chamber Commences Plans to Have its Own Home; Takes Over Fiesta," The Santa Fe New Mexican, June 26, 1920, 6.
307. "Fiesta Notes," The Santa Fe New Mexican, July 31, 1920, 2.
308. "Fiesta Notes," The Santa Fe New Mexican, July 26, 1920, 6.
309. "Fiesta Notes," The Santa Fe New Mexican, August 8, 1920, 4.
310. Ibid., 4.
311. "Fiesta Notes," The Santa Fe New Mexican, August 12, 1920, 2.
312. "Coming Over the Lake Peak Trail to the Fiesta; Big Sombreros Secured by Twitchell in El Paso," The Santa Fe New Mexican, August 16, 1920, 6.
313. "Fiesta Climax Tonight In Dramatic Trial Of Pueblo Plotters," The Santa Fe New Mexican, September 14, 1920, 1.
314. Ibid., 1.
315. Ibid., 1.
316. Ibid., 1.
317. "Fiesta Notes," The Santa Fe New Mexican, August 11, 1920, 6.
318. Ibid., 6.
319. "Fiesta Notes," The Santa Fe New Mexican, August 13, 1920, 7.
320. Ibid., 7.
321. "Col. Twitchell, Author and Publicist, Dies," Joplin Globe, August 27, 1925, 3.
322. "Fiesta resurged in '20s as a tourist attraction," The Santa Fe New Mexican, September 5, 1999, F8.
323. "Fiesta Notes," The Santa Fe New Mexican, September 10, 1920, 3.
324. "Time Turns Back For Three Centuries," The Santa Fe New Mexican, September 13, 1920, 1.
325. "Fiesta resurged in '20s as a tourist attraction," F8.
326. "Santa Fe Fiesta Can Be Made Self-Supporting Institution; Twitchell would Double Seating Capacity For Next Year's Event," The Santa Fe New Mexican, October 21, 1920, 2.
327. "Final Reports Show Fiesta Was Great Success; Col. Twitchell Unanimously Re-Elected Director," The Santa Fe New Mexican, September 22, 1920, 5.
328. "35,000 Printed Boosts Cost City Nothing; Money All Spent At Home," The Santa Fe New Mexican, August 9, 1921, 2.
329. "Visitors from 31 States At The Santa Fe Fiesta," The Santa Fe New Mexican, October 3, 1921, 4.
330. "Fiesta Report Shows Less Than $500," The Santa Fe New Mexican, October 11, 1921, 2.
331. "Friends to Present Painting Tonight to Col. Twitchell, Chief Spirit of the Fiesta," The Santa Fe New Mexican, October 14, 1921, 1.
332. "Col. Twitchell Quits job as president of the Chamber," The Santa Fe New Mexican, February 11, 1922, 1.
333. Ibid., 1.
334a. Ibid., 1.
334b. Ibid., 1.
335. Ibid., 1.
336. "The Fiesta," The Santa Fe New Mexican, February 28, 1922, 4.

337. "Santa Fe Community Spirit Rampant At Fiesta Dinner Last Night; Tremendous Possibilities Of Indian Fair Are Recognized By Boosters," The Santa Fe New Mexican, September 20, 1922, 3.

338. "Cassidy Fiesta Postcards Unique Community Advertising," The Santa Fe New Mexican, August 15, 1922, 4.

339. "Magnificent," The Santa Fe New Mexican, September 5, 1922, 4.

340. "Gate Receipts of Fiesta Are More Than Last Year," The Santa Fe New Mexican, September 8, 1922, 7.

341. "Santa Fe Community Spirit Rampant At Fiesta Dinner Last Night; Tremendous Possibilities Of Indian Fair Are Recognized By Boosters," The Santa Fe New Mexican, September 20, 1922, 3.

342. Ibid., 3.

343. "Society," Albuquerque Morning Journal, March 25, 1925, 5.

344. "Spreading the News," The Santa Fe New Mexican, September 2, 1922, 4.

345. "The Fiesta," The Santa Fe New Mexican, September 3, 1921, 2.

346. "Gate Receipts of Fiesta Are More Than Last Year," The Santa Fe New Mexican, September 8, 1922, 7.

347. The Fiesta organization was actually completely out of debt following the 1923 exposition: see "Fiesta Management Pays All Debts And Has $16 Balance," The Santa Fe New Mexican, September 27, 1923, 7.

348. "Fiesta resurged in '20s as a tourist attraction," F8.

349. Jenkins, "A Dedication to the Memory of Ralph Emerson Twitchell," 104.

350. "Colonel Ralph E. Twitchell Dies In Los Angeles and State Mourns Brilliant Barrister, Historian," 4.

351. "Arid Lands," Los Angeles Times, September 16, 1891, 1.

352. Ibid., 1.

353. "It's Immense!" Las Vegas Daily Optic, March 16, 1892.

354. "Irrigation Convention," Las Vegas Daily Optic, February 6, 1892, 2.

355. "Former Mayor of Santa Fe Called: New Mexico Leader Dies In Hospital," Los Angeles Times, August 27, 1925, A-1.

356. Padilla, "Coronel Ralph E. Twitchell," 3.

357. "Great Congress of Irrigationists Convenes Today: New Mexico Crowd Talks," Salt Lake Tribune, September 15, 1903, 3.

358. "Great Display of Western Fruits," Salt Lake Tribune, September 9, 1903, 1.

359. "Sacramento Will Get The Convention," Reno Evening Gazette, September 6, 1906, 1.

360. "New Mexico Farmers Bring About Deal to Relinquish Reservoir to Texas" Water and Wastes Digest http://www.wwdmag.com/new-mexico-farmers-bring-about-deal-to-relinquish-reservoir-water-texas (May 1, 2003).

361. "Former Mayor of Santa Fe Called: New Mexico Leader Dies in Hospital," A-1.

362. "Will 'Boost' Meadow City," Las Vegas Daily Optic, August 22, 1907, 1.

363. Ibid., 1.

364. Ibid., 1.

365. "Andrews and the Irrigation Congress," Farmington Enterprise, June 26, 1908, 4.

366. "Work That Tells," The Santa Fe New Mexican, February 11, 1908, 2.
367. Padilla, "Coronel Ralph E. Twitchell," 3.
368. "Andrews and the Irrigation Congress," Farmington Enterprise, June 26, 1908, 4.
369. "Albuquerque Should Appreciate," The Santa Fe New Mexican, June 4, 1908, 2.
370. Ibid., 2.
371. Bloom and Walter, "Ralph Emerson Twitchell," 79.
372. "Enlists Aid of Many Hundreds of Newspapers," The Santa Fe New Mexican, February 10, 1908, 1.
373. Jenkins, "A Dedication to the Memory of Ralph Emerson Twitchell," 104.
374. Bloom and Walter, "Ralph Emerson Twitchell," 79.
375. The Santa Fe New Mexican, January 18, 1908, 2.
376. "Mass Meeting at Town Hall," Farmington Enterprise, March 13, 1908, 1.
377. Ibid., 1.
378. "Doings of the Week in and About Our Town," Rio Grande Republican, May 2, 1908, 5.
379. "Boosting For The Irrigation Congress," The Santa Fe New Mexican, July 30, 1908, 1.
380. "Denver Papers Boost Congress," The Santa Fe New Mexican, January 28, 1908, 14.
381. "Good Work By Twitchell," Rio Grande Republican, June 27, 1908, 4.
382. "The Credit Belongs to Andrews Solely," The Santa Fe New Mexican, July 6, 1908, 2.
383. "New Mexico used Irrigation Spectacle of 1908 to Advance Statehood," The Santa Fe New Mexican, April 23, 2005, B1, B4.
384. "Boosting For The Irrigation Congress," The Santa Fe New Mexican, July 30, 1908, 1.
385. "New Mexico used Irrigation Spectacle of 1908 to Advance Statehood," B1.
386. Ibid., B4.
387. "An Important Congress," Washington Post, May 13, 1908, 6.
388. Ibid., 6.
389. "State Heads Arrive," Washington Post, May 11, 1908, 1.
390. "Governors and Other Representatives of States at White House Conference," Syracuse Herald, May, 14, 1908, 3.
391. "State Heads Arrive," 1.
392. "Governors and Other Representatives of States at White House Conference," 3.
393. "Conservation Conferences," www.theodore-roosevelt.com/images/trenvpics/conservationconferences.pdf.
394. "Want 50,000,000 For Irrigation," Galveston Daily News, August 14, 1909, 1.
395. "Eighteenth National Irrigation Congress," Rio Grande Republican, June 17, 1910, 5.
396. Ibid., 5.
397. "State Control Opens Breach in Convention," Indianapolis Sun, September 26, 1910, 7.
398. "Irrigation Congress," Farmington Enterprise, October 7, 1910, 1.
399. Ibid., 1.
400. Bloom and Walter, "Ralph Emerson Twitchell," 79.
401. "Distinguished Visitor," Arizona Republican, April 5, 1911, 6.
402. "Irrigation Congress May Be Postponed," Salt Lake Tribune, May 6, 1913, 14.
403. "Governor Names Many Delegates," The Santa Fe New Mexican, August 10, 1915, 5.
404. Fauntleroy, "Ralph Emerson Twitchell Took on Large Orders," 1.

405. "New Mexico to Have Exhibit on Coast," Rio Grande Republican, April 22, 1910, 3.

406. Bloom and Walter, "Ralph Emerson Twitchell," 79.

407. Padilla, "Coronel Ralph E. Twitchell," 4.

408. Ibid., 4.

409. Ibid., 4.

410. Richard Amero, "History of the Balboa Park Club / New Mexico Building in Balboa Park," San Diego History Center www.sandiegohistory.org/bpbuildings/newmex.htm.

411. John MacGregor, "State's Panama-Pacific Building Reconstructed on Santa Fe Plaza," The Santa Fe New Mexican, November 5, 1967, D1,D2.

412. Caffey, Frank Springer and New Mexico, 184.

413. "Can't Boost Unless There's A Change In City Methods, Says Twitchell," 4.

414. "In Old Santa Fe: 50 Years Ago," Santa Fe Daily New Mexican, August 28, 1962, 22.

415. Richard Amero, "History of the Balboa Park Club / New Mexico Building in Balboa Park," San Diego History Center, www.sandiegohistory.org/bpbuildings/newmex.htm.

416. "Unique Exhibit At San Diego," Deming Headlight, May 1, 1914, 1.

417. Bloom and Walter, "Ralph Emerson Twitchell," 80.

418. Fauntleroy, "Ralph Emerson Twitchell Took On Large Orders," 1.

419. "Pasatiempo," The Santa Fe New Mexican, February 3, 2006, 53.

420. "Auditorium To Bring Crowds To State Building," Rio Grande Republic, January 1, 1915, 1.

421. "Beautiful New Mexico Building Embodiment of Spirit of Sunshine State, Says Governor," The Santa Fe New Mexican, May 7, 1915, 5.

422. Ibid., 5.

423. Ibid., 5.

424. "Auditorium To Bring Crowds To State Building," 1.

425. "Roosevelt Has Bully Time At Big Show; Much Delighted With New Mexico Building," The Santa Fe New Mexican, July 31, 1915, 3.

426. Ibid., 3.

427. Padilla, "Coronel Ralph E. Twitchell," 4.

428. MacGregor, "State's Panama-Pacific Building Reconstructed on Santa Fe Plaza," D1.

429. "Advertising the Sunshine State," Deming Headlight, August 28, 1914, 6.

430. Richard Melzer, "Panama-California Exposition," New Mexico: A Celebration of the Land of Enchantment (Layton, Utah: Published by Gibbs Smith, 2011), 186.

431. Bloom and Walter, "Ralph Emerson Twitchell," 80.

432. Matthew F. Bokovoy, The San Diego World's Fairs and Southwestern Memory, 1880–1940 (Albuquerque: University of New Mexico Press, 2005), 132-134.

433. Ibid., 132-134.

434. Ibid., 132-134.

435. Ibid., 134.

436. "New Mexico State News," Farmington Times-Hustler, February 15, 1917, 1.

437. Richard Amero "History of the Balboa Park Club / New Mexico Building in Balboa Park," San Diego History Center, www.sandiegohistory.org/bpbuildings/newmex.htm.

438. MacGregor, "State's Panama-Pacific Building Reconstructed on Santa Fe Plaza," D1, D2.

439. Gussie Fauntleroy, "Museum was a much-touted gem for young state," The Santa Fe New Mexican, May 16, 1999, F1.

440. MacGregor, "State's Panama-Pacific Building Reconstructed on Santa Fe Plaza," D1, D2.

441. "Can't Boost Unless There's A Change In City Methods, Says Twitchell," 4.

442. "Justice R. H. Hanna Elected President of Chamber of Commerce at Annual Meet," 5.

443. "50 Percent of Visitors at San Diego Think We Are Old Mexico," The Santa Fe New Mexican, April 17, 1916, 4.

444a. "Col. Twitchell Paints Wonders of New Mexico, Along Historic Trails of State," The Santa Fe New Mexican, February 24, 1917, 2.

444b. "Annual Good Roads Meeting," The Rio Grande Republic, August 6, 1915, 1.

444c. "Three Hundred Delegates At Good Roads Meeting; Councils Formally Open This Afternoon," The Santa Fe New Mexican, July 30, 1914, 1.

445. The Santa Fe New Mexican, November 12, 1912, 3.

446. Bloom and Walter, "Ralph Emerson Twitchell," 80, 81.

447. "Santa Fe's Old Civilization," San Antonio Light, September 24, 1911, 14.

448. Simmons, "The Story Behind New Mexico History Author."

449. Richard Flint and Shirley Cushing Flint, "Ralph Emerson Twitchell (1859–1925)," New Mexico Office of the State Historian, http://newmexicohistory.org/filedetails.php?file ID=21280, 2.

450. Ibid., 2.

451. "Post Office Gossip," The Santa Fe New Mexican Review, February 14, 1884, 4.

452. Flint and Flint, "Ralph Emerson Twitchell," 2.

453. Ralph Emerson Twitchell, The Bench and Bar of New Mexico During the American Occupation A.D. 1846–1850 (New Mexican Printing Company, 1891), iv-3.

454. "Business of the Lawyers," Santa Fe Daily New Mexican, January 7, 1891, 5.

455. Ibid., 5.

456. "History of American Occupation," Rio Grande Republican, January 30, 1909, 4.

457. Ralph E. Twitchell, "Some Short Speeches," The Ralph Twitchell Collection, Fray Angelico Chavez History Library and Photo Archives, Santa Fe.

458. Ralph E. Twitchell, "The Public School," The Ralph Twitchell Collection, Fray Angelico Chavez History Library and Photo Archives, Santa Fe.

459. Bloom and Walter, "Ralph Emerson Twitchell," 80.

460. Ibid., 80.

461. Jenkins, "A Dedication to the Memory of Ralph Emerson Twitchell," 105.

462. Simmons, "The Story Behind New Mexico History Author," C-1, C-3.

463. Ibid., C-1, C-3.

464. Jenkins, "A Dedication to the Memory of Ralph Emerson Twitchell," 105,106.

465. "A New Work By Twitchell," Las Vegas Daily Optic, February 11, 1914, 4.

466. Ibid., 4.

467. Ibid., 4.

468. Ibid., 4.

469. "Spanish Archives Will Be Sent to Members of House and Newspapers," The Santa Fe New Mexican, January 29, 1915, 5.
470. Simmons, "The Story Behind New Mexico History Author," C-1, C-3.
471. "History of American Occupation," 4.
472. "50 Years Ago," The Santa Fe New Mexican, March 21, 1961, 9.
473. Flint and Flint, "Ralph Emerson Twitchell," 2.
474. Jenkins, "A Dedication to the Memory of Ralph Emerson Twitchell," 105.
475. Flint and Flint, "Ralph Emerson Twitchell," 2.
476. "Twitchell's History," Farmington Enterprise, August 23, 1912, 8.
477. Ibid., 8.
478. Jenkins, "A Dedication to the Memory of Ralph Emerson Twitchell," 105.
479. Simmons, "The Story Behind N. M. History Author," C-1, C-3.
480. "Colonel Twitchell," Albuquerque Morning Journal, August 28, 1925, 6.
481. "Twitchell's History," 8.
482. "Colonel Twitchell," 6.
483. "Recalls Big Hoax," 1.
484. "Roberts and Twitchell Write Text Book," Deming Headlight, August 21, 1914, 4.
485. "Las Vegas Normal Grows," Deming Headlight, August 28, 1914, 2.
486. "Ralph Emerson Twitchell," El Palacio, 86.
487. Twitchell, Genealogy, 446.
488. "Estelle Bennett Twitchell," El Palacio, 361.
489. Bloom and Walter, "Ralph Emerson Twitchell," 81.
490. "Article on Santa Fe," The Santa Fe New Mexican, September 30, 1916, 5.
491. Ralph E. Twitchell, "Stage Driver to Railroad President," The Santa Fe Magazine, vol. XVII, no. 2, January 1923, 49-51.
492. Twitchell, Genealogy, 446.
493. Bloom and Walter, "Ralph Emerson Twitchell," 81.
494. "Ralph Emerson Twitchell," El Palacio, 86.
495. Jenkins, "A Dedication to the Memory of Ralph Emerson Twitchell," 105.
496. "Ralph Emerson Twitchell," El Palacio, 86.
497. Twitchell, Genealogy, V.
498. "Ralph Emerson Twitchell," El Palacio, 84.
499. Twitchell, Genealogy, lxi.
500. Ibid., V-VII.
501. "Down The Old Santa Fe Trail, 50 Years Ago: From the files of The New Mexican, March 13, 1919," The Santa Fe New Mexican, March 13, 1974, 34.
502. "Down The Old Santa Fe Trail, 25 Years Ago: From the files of The New Mexican, May 16, 1949," The Santa Fe New Mexican, May 16, 1974, 80.
503. Flint and Flint, "Ralph Emerson Twitchell," 2.
504. Jenkins, "A Dedication to the Memory of Ralph Emerson Twitchell," 105.
505. Ibid., 105.
506. Ibid., 105.
507. Ibid., 105.

508. Ibid., 106.

509. Padilla, "Coronel Ralph E. Twitchell," 6.

510. "He Was Famous In Southwest," Reno Evening Gazette, August 26, 1925, 6.

511. "Colonel Ralph E. Twitchell Dies In Los Angeles and State Mourns Brilliant Barrister, Historian," 1.

512. Ibid., 1.

513. Ibid., 1.

514. "Ralph Emerson Twitchell," El Palacio, 83.

515. "Colonel Ralph E. Twitchell Dies In Los Angeles and State Mourns Brilliant Barrister, Historian," 1.

516. Ibid., 1.

517. Ibid., 1.

518. Ibid., 1.

519. Ibid., 1.

520. "Letter from Waldo Twitchell to Lansing Bloom," August 3, 1925, Ralph E. Twitchell Papers, New Mexico State Records Center and Archives, Santa Fe.

521. Ibid.

522. Ibid.

523. Ibid.

524. "Letter from Waldo Twitchell to Lansing Bloom," August 9, 1925, Ralph E. Twitchell papers, New Mexico State Records Center and Archives, Santa Fe.

525. Ibid.

526. Ibid.

527. Ibid.

528. "Ralph Emerson Twitchell," El Palacio, 83.

529. "Colonel Ralph E. Twitchell Dies In Los Angeles and State Mourns Brilliant Barrister, Historian," 1.

530. Ibid., 1.

531. Ibid., 1.

532. Ibid., 1.

533. Ibid., 1.

534. "Bury Col. Twitchell at Cross of Martyrs," Roswell Daily Record, August 28, 1925, 4.

535. "Last Rights for Col. Twitchell at 3 Sunday," August 28, 1925, Ralph E. Twitchell Collection, New Mexico State Records Center and Archives, Santa Fe.

536. "Funeral of Twitchell to be Held in Santa Fe Sunday Afternoon," Albuquerque Morning Journal, August 28, 1925, 1.

537. "Last Rights for Col. Twitchell at 3 Sunday," August 28, 1925, Ralph E. Twitchell Collection.

538. "Hewett's Brother Dead," Albuquerque Morning Journal, August 29, 1925, 3.

539. Ibid.

540. "Hundreds Pay Meed of Love and Respect to Twitchell," The Santa Fe New Mexican, August 31, 1925.

541. "Twitchell is Given Tribute by New Mexico," Albuquerque Morning Journal, August 31, 1925, 1.

542. Ibid., 1.

543. Ibid., 1.

544. "Hundreds Pay Meed of Love and Respect to Twitchell," The Santa Fe New Mexican, August 31, 1925.

545. Ibid.

546. "Twitchell is Given Tribute by New Mexico," Albuquerque Morning Journal, August 31, 1925, 1.

547. Ibid., 1.

548. "Urge Monument For Twitchell," The Santa Fe New Mexican, September 2, 1925.

549. Ibid.

550. "Historical Society Will Hold Memorial for Late Col. Twitchell," The Santa Fe New Mexican, September 12, 1925.

551. "In Old Santa Fe from...The New Mexican 25 Years Ago," The Santa Fe New Mexican, July 26, 1949, 4.

552. Flint and Flint, "Ralph Emerson Twitchell," 3.

553. 1908, 1913, Sanborn Maps of Santa Fe, New Mexico, Sanborn Map Company, http://sanborn.umi.com/sanborn/image/view?state=nm, New Mexico State Library, Southwest Collection.

554. "Pioneers Should Be Remembered By Honoring With Street Names," The Santa Fe New Mexican, December 10, 1952, 4.

555. "Ralph Emerson Twitchell," El Palacio, 87.

556. "Pioneers Should Be Remembered By Honoring With Street Names," 4.

557. "Restore the Old Veranda," The Santa Fe New Mexican, March 7, 1905, 1.

558. "Col. R. E. Twitchell Dies Today; Will Be Buried In Old Santa Fe City," Roswell Daily Record, August 26, 1925, 1.

559. "Waldo: The town and the man," Rio Rancho Observer, January 16, 2005, A-6.

560. "Group adds two names for building," The Santa Fe New Mexican, July 28, 1975, 8.

561. "HSNM SOLICITS AWARD NOMINATIONS," La Cronica de Nuevo Mexico, issue 23, April, 1986, 4.

www.ingramcontent.com/pod-product-compliance
Lightning Source LLC
Chambersburg PA
CBHW021403090426
42742CB00009B/988